RUNNING YOUR RACE

A Christian's Guide to Growing in Christ

Volume I: Agape Love

Camille A. McKenzie

Running Your Race: A Christian's Guide to Growing in Christ. Copyright © 2020. Camille A. McKenzie. All Rights Reserved.

No rights claimed for public domain material. No parts of this publication may be reproduced, stored in any retrieval system, or transmitted in any form or by any means, electronic, mechanical, recording, or otherwise, without the prior written permission of the author. Violations may be subject to civil or criminal penalties.

ISBN: 978-1-953759-08-5 (paperback)

Printed in the United States of America

Unless otherwise indicated, all Scripture quotations are taken from the New American Standard Bible Copyright 1960, 1962, 1963, 1968, 1971, 1972, 1973, 1975, 1977, 1995 by The Lockman Foundation. Used by permission.

To Jesus Christ: the perfect example of agape love.

Acknowledgments

C. Orville McLeish and the team at HCP Book Publishing for their hard work in all aspects of the book creation and publishing process.

Errol Stevens for his recommendation of HCP Book Publishing.

Marlene Oulton for being my faithful wordsmith and making my writing coherent to the world.

John Ssentamu for his suggestion to transcribe my Facebook broadcasts into books.

My husband, Chris McKenzie, for his moral support and education about the actual exercise of running.

Table of Contents

Acknowledgments 5
Introduction 9
    Love and Running Your Race 17
Chapter 1: Agape Love: The Crown Jewel of the Christian Faith **19**
    What is Agape Love? 29
Chapter 2: Agape Love is Patient **39**
    Core Fears 45
Chapter 3: The Fear Dance **51**
    Cultivating Patience 53
Chapter 4: Love is Kind **61**
    Love is Not Envious 65
Chapter 5: Love is Not Arrogant **73**
    Love is Not Rude 77
Chapter 6: Love is Humble **83**
    Love Has Amnesia 87
Chapter 7: Love Rejoices with the Truth **91**
    Love and Service 94
Chapter 8: Love Bears All Things **97**
    Love Believes All Things 100

Chapter 9: Love Hopes All Things **105**
    Love Endures All Things 110
Chapter 10: Live Like You Are Loved **117**
    Father's Love Letter 119
The Prodigal Son Story 123
About the Author 129

Introduction

"Therefore, since we have so great a cloud of witnesses surrounding us, let us also lay aside every encumbrance and the sin which so easily entangles us, and let us run with endurance the race that is set before us, fixing our eyes on Jesus, the author and perfecter of faith, who for the joy set before Him endured the cross, despising the shame, and has sat down at the right hand of the throne of God." – Hebrews 12:1-2

Imagine yourself in this scene:

"The unremitting road stretches on endlessly into the scorched and blurred horizon. A sweltering heat pulsates all around as tattered shoes, seasoned by hundreds of miles, pound into the dirt one blistering stride after another. You feel each excruciating muscle taxed of all energy and effort. Every breath screams desperate for another ounce of oxygen. Every continued heartbeat is a miracle as the rhythm in your chest echoes with the thuds of your feet hitting the ground…" – [1]

---

[1] https://www.goodnewsfl.org/extraordinary-tells-inspiring-true-story-family-faith/

How would you be feeling? I am sure, like myself, every ounce of you would want to give up and quit. You are tired. During the race, you have had moments of victory and triumph, but the sheer nature of the race has been exhausting. There were many times you had to push yourself to go on. The distance you have been running is long, and you are uncertain that you have enough within you to finish your race. This, my friend, is the reality of running a race.

In Hebrews 12:1-2, the apostle Paul, inspired by the Holy Spirit, describes the Christian's journey as a race. What a perfect metaphor for the Christian life! Paul has used the race metaphor in other places of Scripture which makes the metaphor highly significant (See 2 Timothy 4:7, 1 Corinthians 9:24-25, Acts 20:24).

I believe the apostle Paul was inspired to use this metaphor because the Christian journey requires endurance. Our race is not easy and will not be easy. It requires us to have a mindset of a runner and a soldier. Paul encourages us to join him and endure hardship as good soldiers of Christ (See 2 Timothy 2:3).

In 2 Timothy 4:7, the apostle makes three powerful statements that represent his victory in winning *his race*: "I have fought the good fight, I have finished the race, I have kept the faith" (2 Timothy 4:7). How do we become victorious like the Apostle Paul and win our race? Well, Paul tells us how in our text, Hebrews 12:1-2. He mentions four things we need to do:

1. Lay aside every encumbrance;
2. Lay aside the sin in our lives;
3. Run with endurance;
4. Fix our eyes on Jesus.

The apostle first tells us two things that we need to avoid (encumbrances and sin) and two things that we must actively pursue (running with endurance and fixing our eyes on Jesus). The first thing Paul instructs us to do is to lay aside encumbrances in our lives. So, what exactly is an encumbrance (some translations use weights)? An encumbrance can be defined as a bulk or a mass: it is anything that hinders or prevents us from doing something or making progress.

Encumbrances or weights can be innocent and harmless but can still impact our race as a Christian. Encumbrances could be watching a lot of T.V. and videos, accumulating many material possessions, relationships, our careers, our need for respect or approval, or our need to be liked by others. An encumbrance can also be good deeds that, while noble, are taking us away from the core mission that God has called us to do.

In Gary Thomas' book, *When to Walk Away*, he gives an excellent example of how good deeds can become encumbrances from running our specific race:

"If I send an employee to a gas station to fill the gas tank of a company car and they return to the office saying, 'I had a great conversation

with Skip. I washed the windshield. I picked up some litter in the parking lot, and I even brought back donuts for the entire office, but he didn't fill the gas tank, has he really been obedient? He may have done some good and noble things, but those other things got in the way of the first thing." [2]

Clearly, we are commanded to do good deeds and to serve others. But we simply cannot serve everyone all the time and do every good deed that is presented before us. The hardest decisions are not between what is good and bad. Those are relatively easy choices for a Christian. The most heart-wrenching decisions are between two good options for service. In such times we need prayer, wisdom, and discernment. The reality is, as runners for Christ, we will have to make difficult choices to preserve our mission and run our race.

Or what if we are running our race and encounter another kind of encumbrance — people who oppose us, dislike us, lie about us? What do we do then? The words of H. M. Richards provide sound counsel for us in this matter:

"The Lord has given to every man his work. It is his business to do it and the devil's business to hinder him if he can. So surely as God has given you a work to do, Satan will try to hinder you. Keep about your work that God has given you. Do not flinch because the lion roars; Do not stop to stone the devil's dogs; Do not fool away your time chasing

---

[2] Gary Thomas. *When to Walk Away* (p. 61). Zondervan. Kindle Edition.

the devil's rabbits. Let liars lie, let corporations resolve, let the devil do his worst; But see to it that nothing hinders you from fulfilling the work that God has given you. He has not commanded you to get rich. He has never bidden you to defend your character. He has not set you at work to contradict falsehoods about yourself, which Satan and his servants may start to peddle. If you do those things, you will do nothing else. You will be at work for yourself and not the Lord. Let your aim be as steady as a star. You may be assaulted, wronged, insulted, slandered, wounded, and rejected; you may be abused by foes, forsaken by friends, and despised and rejected of men. But see to it with steadfast determination, with unfaltering zeal, that you pursue the great purpose of your life and object of your being until at last you can say: 'I have finished the work which you gave me to do!'"

It is worth noting here that it is not really until you run your race, seeking to fulfill your purpose, that you will be viciously attacked by the enemy. The message by H. M. Richards and the Apostle Paul is the same: keep focused on your race and win it. By the way you can't know your encumbrances in a vacuum. It is only by running your race that you will gain keen insight to what is actually encumbering you. My friends, I ask you, what do you need to lay aside to run your race without impediments?

The second thing that we need to lay aside is sin. Sin, just like encumbrances, can entangle us and completely destroy our ability to run our race. We must make a clear decision that we will fight sin within us at every turn with the power of God so that it does not hinder our race. What are some of the sins that we need to lay aside? Some of the sins we can lay aside is falsehood (See Ephesians 4:25), anger, wrath, malice, slander, and abusive speech (See Colossians 3:8), filthiness (See James 1:21), and hypocrisy, envy, and guile (See 1 Peter 2:1) to name a few.

Paul next mentions a quality that is necessary for us to possess as we run — endurance. In running our race, we will encounter resistance, both internal and external. Internal resistance deals with our mindset. As you are running, what are you telling yourself when it gets hard, when it seems like you aren't making progress? How do you handle the moments of the race when you want to give up and quit? What is your inspiration to keep running to the finish line? To win our race we must have an Olympic athlete's mindset of intense focus upon our goal and a relentless desire to win and not to quit. Like an Olympic athlete, a Christian runner must train our bodies, emotions, mind, and every faculty of our being so that we can win our heavenly prize (See 1 Corinthians 9:27, Philippians 3:14).

Arthur Pink makes this point well when he noted:

"The principal thoughts suggested by the figure of the 'race' are rigorous self-denial and discipline, vigorous exertion, persevering endurance. The Christian life is not a thing of passive luxury, but of active 'fighting the good fight of faith!' The Christian is not called to lie down on flowery beds of ease, but to run a race, and athletics are

strenuous, demanding self-sacrifice, hard training, the putting forth of every ounce of energy possessed." ³

In addition to overcoming internal resistance, a Christian runner must overcome the external resistance we will face. External resistance is about all the circumstances of life that will happen to you as you are running your race. External resistance can take the form of relational issues, illness, financial issues, stressful life responsibilities, spiritual attacks, etc. It may feel, at times, like life is conspiring against you in your desire to win your race for Christ. As you are making progress toward the things that God has called you to do, life will start happening around you. Challenges will come out of nowhere; left, and right. This is when you must go back to a winner's mindset, and remember your motivation for finishing and winning your race.

The apostle Paul gives two sources of inspiration and motivation — the great cloud of witnesses (See Hebrews 11), and Jesus the author and finisher of our faith (See Hebrews 12:2). The great cloud of witnesses reminds us that while the race is hard, like them, we can win with our primary source of motivation: Jesus Christ. Friedrich Nietzsche said that: *"He who has a why to live for can bear almost any how."* When we keep our eyes, our focus, fixed on why we are running our race when the hard times come, we will endure, we will fight to finish. Jesus

---

³Arthur W. Pink. *An Exposition of Hebrews* (Arthur Pink Collection Book 21). Prisbrary Publishing. Kindle Edition.

provides not only the source of our inspiration but our example as well. As we look upon Jesus and how He ran His race, we are inspired to continue to run ours no matter how difficult it may be. In the end, we are running our race to please Jesus.

Let us now turn our attention to what **running your race is not:**

- ∝ Running your race is not a competition against others (unlike earthly races). It is about running YOUR race with all your might. You have no competition: you are running against yourself. Do not compare yourself to others and their progress in their race. Keep focused on your lane and run your race well.

- ∝ Running your race is not about speed and how fast you run. Your race is like a marathon. It is about enduring the long distance and running until the end. It is about training well and learning the lessons you have to learn so you can finish your race. If you get tired, slow down a little, but do not quit.

- ∝ Running your race is not about perfection. It is about living in the love of God and knowing your Father's heart towards you. You are going to fail. You are going to make mistakes. You are going to want to give up and quit. You are going to feel as if you are not doing things right. But when you know the heart of your Father and

His immense love for you, then you have the strength and courage you need to keep running.

∝ Running your race is not about one winner. We are *all* winners if we finish the race of our lives by honoring and glorifying God and Jesus Christ.

Love and Running Your Race

When we speak of running our race for Christ, while we are called to fulfill our specific purpose, at the center of our race is our relationships. The Christian life is played out in our relationships. In Matthew 22:37-40, Jesus said, "…You shall love the Lord your God with all your heart, and with all your soul, and with all your mind." This is the great and foremost commandment. The second is like it, "You shall love your neighbor as yourself." On these two commandments depend the whole Law and the Prophets." Loving God and others become one of the chief measurements of what it means to run our race and to finish well.

Love is not how the world defines it. We often hear someone say that they love ice cream in the same sentence that they say they love someone. Love is not just a word we throw around. Agape love is a special love that represents the heart of the triune God's character. 1 Corinthians 13:1-8 defines true love. As Ray Pritchard noted, *"The Apostle Paul now begins to describe what love looks like. Verses 4-8 contain 15 short phrases that, like a prism held up to the sun, show us the full spectrum of love. Many people think this is the most beautiful and complete statement on love ever written. As we look at these verses, I advise you to buckle up tight because if you take these verses seriously, you are sure to be challenged, convicted, and prodded into a new way of living and a new way of loving."* [4]

In order to experience a new way of living and loving, Jesus must live in our hearts as our Lord and Savior. God wants to take us on a journey for His love to flow through us to others. As we become vessels of God's love, we can change our corner of the world and become healing agents of the Kingdom of God. As you read this book, remember: *"Love difficult people. You are one of them."* – TobyMac

---

[4] http://www.keepbelieving.com/sermon/why-love-has-a-bad-memory/

Chapter 1
Agape Love: The Crown Jewel of the Christian Faith

"Are you alive?" This is an interesting question, isn't it? The apostle Paul asks us to consider this matter in Romans 6:10-13 where he states:

"For the death that He died, He died to sin once for all; but the life that He lives, He lives to God. Even so consider yourselves to be dead to sin, but alive to God in Christ Jesus. Therefore do not let sin reign in your mortal body so that you obey its lusts, and do not go on presenting the members of your body to sin as instruments of unrighteousness; but present yourselves to God as those alive from the dead, and your members as instruments of righteousness to God."

Prior to these verses, Paul wrote:

"Now if we have died with Christ, we believe that we shall also live with Him, knowing that Christ, having been raised from the dead, is never to die again; death no longer is master over Him." (Romans 6:8-9).

Paul is essentially saying that we died when we accepted Jesus Christ as our Lord and Savior. Since we died with Christ, we are alive in Him and can live a righteous life. While our sinful nature is still present, for those who are born from above, the power of sin has been broken. The gift of grace, through Jesus Christ, has given us the power to be alive to God every day – to live for Him. So, I ask you again, "Are you alive?"

Now your answer to that question is largely determined by which lord you are obeying on a day to day basis. Paul makes it clear that on our Christian journey, there are two lords that we could choose to follow. The first lord is sin, which makes us slaves. The second lord is righteousness, which makes us free and servants of righteousness and God.

God is saying to us daily, *"Are you going to choose My way and be a servant of righteousness, or are you going to choose sin? Which one do you want to be: a slave of sin or a servant of righteousness?"*

A major key to living as servants of righteousness and experiencing a victorious life (besides the power of the Holy Spirit) is our mindset – our belief system. Our mindsets determine how we live. The Apostle Paul says, "Consider yourself dead to sin." Before any of us can refuse for sin to reign in our bodies and present our bodies to God as instruments of righteousness, we must think biblically. Instead of thinking, "I can't help my tendency to commit this sin" (whatever it may be), you must KNOW, believe, confess, and think that you are dead to that sin, meaning that sin has no power to control you.

In essence, Paul is saying as it relates to that sin that you are battling, do not see yourself or consider yourself a helpless victim of that sin because you are not. The power of sin is broken when we acknowledge our union with Christ's death to sin (consider ourselves dead to that sin) and our ability to live for God.

The Message version of Romans 6:10-13 makes this point well when it states:

"Could it be any clearer? Our old way of life was nailed to the cross with Christ, a decisive end to that sin-miserable life – no longer at sin's every beck and call! What we believe is this: If we get included in Christ's sin-conquering death, we also get included in his life-saving resurrection. We know that when Jesus was raised from the dead it was a signal of the end of death-as-the-end. Never again will death have the last word. When Jesus died, he took sin down with him, but alive he brings God down to us. From now on, think of it this way: Sin speaks a dead language that means nothing to you; God speaks your mother tongue, and you hang on every word. You are dead to sin and alive to God. That's what Jesus did. That means you must not give sin a vote in the way you conduct your lives.

Don't give it the time of day. Don't even run little errands that are connected with that old way of life. Throw yourselves wholeheartedly and full-time – remember you've been raised from the dead! – into God's way of doing things. Sin can't tell you how to live. After all, you're not living under that old tyranny any longer. You're living in the freedom of God."

These truths are very important for us to remember as we face daily temptations and seek to fulfill our call to love.

In Matthew 22:37-40, Jesus gives us the greatest commandment, which is to love God and our neighbor. This may seem like an impossible command, but the power is within us to choose to be alive to God, servants of righteousness, and live a life of love. Romans 5 reassures us of this truth when it notes "… that hope does not disappoint, because the love of God has been poured out within our hearts through the Holy Spirit who was given to us." (Romans 5:5).

While this is true, why do we struggle to love others as God loves us? What stops the divine nature from flowing out and being manifested in our lives? It is our sinful nature that still exists within us. You can think of it in this way: Agape is flowing through our veins, but the sinful nature can create a blockage to that flow of divine love and grace. However, God will journey with us to remove the blockages of sin and pride within us so agape love can flow freely through us.

In order to partner with God to remove the blockages of sin within our hearts, we need to cultivate four foundational elements: surrender, humility, self-denial, and a hunger for truth.

Surrender – The daily surrender of our hearts and lives to God is necessary to allow God to root out the sins that lie deep within each of us. Most of us know and have sung the famous song *I Surrender All* — but how many of us understand what true surrender is all about?

I love how Andrew Murray describes what absolute surrender looks like. He notes, *"You know in daily life what absolute surrender is. You know that everything has to be given up to its special, definite object and service. I have a pen in my pocket, and that pen is absolutely surrendered to the one work of writing, and that pen must be absolutely surrendered to my hand if I am to write properly with it. If another holds it partly, I cannot write properly. This coat is absolutely given up to me to cover my body. This building is entirely given up to religious services. And now, do you expect that in your immortal being, in the divine nature that you have received by regeneration, God can work His work, every day and every hour, unless you are entirely given up to Him? God cannot. The Temple of Solomon was absolutely surrendered to God when it was dedicated to Him. And every one of us is a temple of God, in which God will dwell and work mightily on one condition – absolute surrender to Him. God claims it, God is worthy of it, and without it God cannot work His blessed work in us."*[5]

Our goal as Christians is to be like a pen, building, or coat, which is completely surrendered to its purpose; in our case, it is to give honor and glory to God – to represent Him in the earth. In order to do so, we must surrender ourselves to God completely – give up our rights to living life on our terms – to live completely on His.

Surrendering will not be easy but remember that He will partner with you on the journey for "It is God that works in us, both to will and to do of his good pleasure." (Philippians 2:13). He will take every experience you encounter and work for your good and those around you. Therefore, you and I need not fear surrendering to God – we are in good hands.

Humility – Andrew Murray wrote that *"pride, or the loss of this humility, is the root of every sin and evil."* I agree. If pride is at the root of every sin and evil, then it stands to reason that humility is at the root of every virtue and righteousness. Without humility, we simply cannot love others, much less live out any other aspect of the Christian life as Christ did.

I firmly believe that any sinful disposition (no matter how dark) can be changed if we possess humility. Conversely, without

---

[5] Andrew Murray, *Humility*. (Minneapolis: Bethany House, 2001), 16.

humility, nothing in our character can be changed, no matter how small. Therefore, humility is one of the keys to growth in the Christian life.

Humility allows us to see and acknowledge our sins and see our personal need for our Savior, Jesus Christ, on a daily basis. This will lead to the daily surrender of our lives to God, prayers for the transformative power of the Holy Spirit, and the clinging to the saving work of Jesus Christ.

I urge you to make humility *"the object of special desire and prayer and faith and practice."* [6] Listen, practically speaking, God will allow various situations in your life to humiliate you, to hit at your "self-esteem" – accept it all as His means to develop this absolute essential quality in your character.

Self-denial – In Matthew 16:24, we read: "Then Jesus said to His disciples, If anyone wishes to come after Me, he must deny himself, and take up his cross and follow Me."

What I love about Christ is that He is radically honest about what it means to be His disciple: to call oneself a Christian, a follower of Christ. Jesus makes it very clear in this verse, and throughout His life with the disciples, that following Him would not be easy. So, if someone says sign me up, *"I am going to be a disciple of Jesus Christ."* Jesus may respond, *"Are you ready*

---

[6] Andrew Murray, *Humility*. (Minneapolis: Bethany House, 2001), 18.

to pay the price of following Me? Are you willing to choose My way of thinking and being over your own? Are you willing to let go of what you may want to do and where you may want to go for Me? Are you willing to let go of any relationship, including your family that is hostile to My will and My way? Are you willing to do battle against your sin nature so I can live through you? Are you willing to suffer for Me and potentially die for me?" These are the kind of questions Christ wants us to answer before we become His disciples.

George Mueller, the great Christian evangelist, understood self-denial well. Mueller said, *"There was a day when I died, utterly died, died to George Mueller, his opinions, preferences, tastes and will, died to the world, its approval or censure, died to the approval or blame even of my brethren and friends, and since then I have studied only to show myself approved unto God."*[7]

Self-denial is absolutely critical in order to manifest agape (love) and the divine life. We cannot follow Christ and fully love God and others if we are full of ourselves and our desires. Our desires, our ways of seeing life, and living life must be crucified in order for Christ's resurrection life – a life of power and righteousness to live within us.

If you are struggling with something, you will not overcome it overnight. But as we practice putting God's will before ours,

---

[7] Quoted in A. T. Pierson, *George Mueller of Bristol: His Life of Prayer and Faith*, pg. 367.

and bringing our inability before God, His power is available to those who humble themselves.

Truth – The New Testament word for truth is defined as reality. In order to experience the transformative power of the Spirit, we must become people who are radically committed to the truth, even the hard truths about ourselves. As Francis Frangipane rightly noted, *"To ascend toward God is to walk into a furnace of truth where falsehood is extracted from our souls. To abide in the holy place we must dwell in honesty, even when a lie might seem to save us. Each ascending step upon the hill of God is a thrusting of our souls into greater transparency, a more perfect view into the motives of our hearts."* [8]

Truth is so important on our road to agape love because it is reality, the way things actually are. If we have a pattern of denying truth about ourselves, others, or truth in the Word of God, agape is impossible. The fact is that we cannot change what we do not acknowledge.

God's Word is our ultimate authority on truth. It is the mirror in which we can see our true selves and also receive the remedy for our sinful patterns.

---

[8] Francis Frangipane, *Holiness, Truth, and the Presence of God*, (Cedar Rapids: Arrow Publications, 2005), 24.

As we commit ourselves to studying and meditating on God's Word, God will reveal the truth about the sin in our lives. When we are faced with truth, God does not want us to become angry (See James 1:19-25), but to humbly accept what He is showing us, repent of sin, and renew our minds (in His Word) so He can change us.

For example, say a wife has been arguing with her husband about not spending enough time with her. She may feel that her angry responses are justified. She may reason, *"Isn't marriage a priority in the Bible? Therefore, I am right in helping my husband to honor his biblical priorities."*

Imagine one day that she is studying the book of Proverbs and comes across Proverbs 14:1, "The wise woman builds her house, But the foolish tears it down with her own hands." A few moments later, she reads Proverbs 25:24, "It is better to live in a corner of the roof than in a house shared with a contentious woman." The wife's heart is touched by the Holy Spirit, and she realizes that her angry yelling sessions with her husband are foolish. She acknowledges the truth of the Word of God that she is destroying her own marriage through her angry reactions. She speaks to God about her past behavior, repents, and asks Him to show her how to live a life of wisdom and love with her husband. She then searches the Bible for wisdom in how to handle her anger in the right way.

This wife will now be on the road to agape love because she has bowed her knees to truth: truth about herself and truth she received from the Word of God.

We must be so committed to truth that even when it comes through a source we do not like, we will receive it. When people speak things to us, take them before God and ask Him, *"Lord, is this true?"* He will reveal whether it is or not. Even when the truth hurts, scares, shames, or humiliates you – admit it, confess it, repent of it, and ask God to change you. Dwell in honesty at all costs. This is the path to humility and to agape – the life of Christ.

So, I ask you, my friend: *"Are you committed to surrendering your daily life to Him? Are you committed to growing in humility? Are you committed to denying yourself, taking up your cross, and following Christ daily? Are you committed to growing in your understanding and application of God's truth?"* If you answer yes, you are well on your way to maturing in love.

What is Agape Love?

What exactly is love? There are several types of love that are expressed in the Word of God. One of those words is phileo, the Greek word for brotherly love. Phileo is the natural, human love we express to others, and it is usually mutual. Jesus says in Matthew 5:46, "For if you love those who love you, what reward do you have? Do not even the tax collectors do the same?" Jesus knew it was natural to be able to love people who love us. But agape is different. Agape is a kind of love that says: "I will seek your highest good. I will seek your best interest. I will sacrifice on your behalf." It doesn't matter if the recipient likes us or not; agape will act in their best interest. Agape chooses to be patient and kind. It chooses not to be self-centered, but other-centered. Agape hopes for the best, sees the best in others and endures the ups and downs of relationships.

This thing called life is a big classroom where God will give us daily opportunities to practice agape. In order to prepare for the challenging relationships that will come our way, renew your mind daily with the truth of God's Word. Love begins in our minds. Read 1 Corinthians 13 daily and keep reflecting upon it. As we do, God will begin to meet us at our point of need in our relationships. His power will become evident to us over a period of time. Humble yourself before God; deny your natural desire to do whatever you want to do and serve God instead. Choose to continue to submit and surrender to His Lordship and not the Lordship of sin.

The divine power of God through Christ Jesus our Lord has set us free, that we can be alive to God and not alive to sin. We have a choice, and God's power is present. Consider His power, claim His power, think about His power, and not your own.

It is a struggle to really love people. We all encounter those people who just rub us the wrong way and provoke an ungodly response. Lucy once said to Charlie Brown, *"The world I love; it's people I can't stand."* The reality is, love operates within the context of human relationships. So, we have to learn how to love all kinds of people because all lives matter to God.

The apostle Paul penned these powerful words that define true love in 1 Corinthians 13:1-8. He wrote:

"If I speak with the tongues of men and of angels, but do not have love, I have become a noisy gong or a clanging cymbal. If I have the gift of prophecy, and know all mysteries and all knowledge; and if I have all faith, so as to remove mountains, but do not have love, I am nothing. And if I give all my possessions to feed the poor, and if I surrender my body to be burned, but do not have love, it profits me nothing. Love is patient, love is kind and is not jealous; love does not brag and is not arrogant, does not act unbecomingly; it does not seek its own, is not provoked, does not take into account a wrong suffered, does not rejoice in unrighteousness, but rejoices with the truth; bears all things, believes all things, hopes all things, endures all things."

Paul confirms that love is eternal, and it will outlast anything we do. If we build on any other foundation except love, what we build will not stand the test of time. Love existed before God created the world, and it will always exist. We can build our lives on so many things, even our spiritual gifts. But the apostle Paul reminds us that while there are great spiritual gifts, even those gifts will not last. Additionally, Paul teaches us that if we do not have love, our gifts, and service to God all count for nothing. So, what are you spending your life doing? Without the crown jewel of the Christian faith, it is meaningless.

Agape love is the identifying quality or mark of a Christian. Jesus made this clear that this is the quality that makes people know that we are His disciples (See John 13:35). Love is not about the extravagant services that we may do. While love serves others, there is a particular approach to relationships that is defined in these verses.

Love is not just about us having a sentiment or an emotion or a feeling about someone. Agape love can include lovely feelings, but true agape love operates in spite of "loving" feelings. Agape love will still operate toward those who hate us. Agape love will still operate toward those who are ungrateful to us or people that may "spit" in our face repeatedly. Agape love chooses, as an act of will, to still seek a person's highest good in spite of the fact that that person may never, ever return our love. That is agape. It is not a natural love that we possess that we can just conjure up. It is poured into the hearts of disciples of Christ, by God's Spirit.

There are eight qualities that define agape love. Let us call them the positives of love. Love is defined as being patient, kind, being happy with truth, protective over another's reputation, believes the best about others, hopeful in all things, willing to endure the tough things, and love never gives up.

I want you to take a quick inventory of your love life: are you patient? Are you kind? Do you have a problem with the truth and being happy when the truth comes in your life or the life of others? Are you someone who is quick to gossip about other people? Are you quick to tell others what they have done wrong? Do you believe the best about people, or do you tend to believe the worst? Are you hopeful in your relationships? Are you willing to endure, or are you quick to bail out and quit in your relationships?

Paul was inspired to also list for us the negatives of love – in other words, what true biblical love is not. Love is not envious; some translations say jealous. It really means envy. Love does not brag. Love is not arrogant. Love does not act unbecomingly. Love does not seek its' own. Love is not easily provoked. Love does not keep a record of what people have done. Love does not rejoice in wrong. It is not celebratory when things are wrong (See 1 Corinthians 13:4-8).

Do you notice a common trait about the negatives of love? I challenge you to look again if you do not initially see it. The common trait that connects all the negatives of love is a focus on "I." Love is not self-centered and focused on "me, myself and I." True love is other-centered and is consistently focused on others.

Time for another inventory of your soul. What areas in your life is God seeking to work on? Do you see arrogance as an issue for you? Are you someone who is easily provoked? Are you someone who keeps the list of the things that people have done against you? Where are you on this list?

All the negative attributes of love that Paul talks about, for example, bragging, arrogance, etc. can create huge problems in our relationships. We cannot practice agape when those things are present. However, God can give us the power to break through our patterns of lovelessness so we can grow in love and love others as He loves them.

Now let us look at some steps we can follow to allow agape love to flow freely through us.

Step One: Place your relationships into two categories: the God box and your box.

What are the things that you can control in your relationships? Those things go into your box. What are the things that you cannot control? Those things go into God's box. For example, you cannot control the actions and decisions of a drug-addicted family member who refuses to get treatment. However, you can pray for them and be there for them when they are ready to go into a recovery program.

In other words, your job is to live a life of love by continuing to do positive actions towards that person. Loving that drug-addicted relative is choosing to be slow to get angry with the person. It is choosing to believe the best about the person, hoping for the best outcome for them, being willing to not give up on them.

As we surrender the situation and person before God, commit to stop worrying about it, and trust that God will take care of the person. Agape really shines when we love in this way. Agape love makes people take notice of it. The world will want to know how on earth we can still love that person (agape) with all that is going on in their life.

Step Two: Accept the person and the situation for what it is.

We are gracious recipients of God's acceptance. He knows us, yet He accepts us. Likewise, we need to accept others for where they are on their journey. If you do not accept them, you are always going to be in a mode of trying to change them, and that is God's job. Yes, there are some things that we can do, but it is not our job to change people. God is the one who will do that.

Step Three: Lower your expectations.

This is a huge step. Our expectations, desires, wants, what we expect from people; all these need to come from one person only, and that is God. When we have a lot of expectations of a person or a relationship, this will create distress and relational conflict. I love the quote that says, *"Expectations are premeditated resentment."*

While we may have godly expectations of what we know a person should be doing, again, we cannot change another human being. We can influence them through our words and through our actions, but they make the decisions as to whether or not they want to change. We cannot compel them. We cannot grab them by the scruff of their neck, and we cannot force them to do what we want them to do. So, lower your expectations.

With a lowered expectation of human beings, preferably lowered to zero, you decrease your stress, and you are able to be patient. Simply said: put your hope in God, not in man.

Step Four: Cultivate a godly perspective of others.

Choose to believe the best about people and not the worst. Choose to hope for the best to happen in your relationships and in the life of others. We must look at the positives about the person instead of thinking about all the things they have done wrong, particularly against us.

Change your perspective so that it reflects how God would view this person. God never focuses on what is wrong about someone. He focuses on what is right. He focuses on His grace operating in someone's life, which generates hope. We must surrender our perspective to God so that it reflects His.

Step Five: Deal with yourself.

If you are someone who gets irritated easily, you need to evaluate why things bother you. We need to evaluate why things get us angry in our relationships. We need to get to the root cause.

What often triggers our lack of patience ultimately comes back to our self-centeredness. For example, imagine that someone says that you are ugly. If you do not believe that you are ugly, it will not impact you emotionally. But suppose that same person says to you that you are too short, and you have an issue with your height. Now you find yourself getting upset. You are responding to that person with defensiveness and anger.

The root issue is really in you and not in them. The problem here is that what the person said about you is really how you see yourself. The person did not push your buttons when they said you were ugly because you do not see yourself that way. But they were able to push your buttons because you saw yourself as being too short. Therefore, your response to that person was unloving because of your beliefs.

We need to deal with ourselves because this becomes the greatest roadblock towards being able to demonstrate agape love in the world and in our relationships. As God removes our internal roadblocks, His love can more easily flow through us.

Chapter 2
Agape Love is Patient

Are you a murderer? Consider this question in light of the fact that Christ linked anger with murder in Matthew 5:21-26. The Apostle James did the same in the book of James. In James 4:1-3, we read:

"What is the source of quarrels and conflicts among you? Is not the source your pleasures that wage war in your members? You lust and do not have; so you commit murder. You are envious and cannot obtain; so you fight and quarrel. You do not have because you do not ask. You ask and do not receive, because you ask with wrong motives, so that you may spend it on your pleasures."

What is James saying to us here? It is very important to understand. James wants us to see that the source of our anger is often internal.

Edward Welch rightly noted: *"We were minding our own business — not angry — and someone comes along and makes us angry. We* were not angry before; we became angry after. If that other person had acted in a different way, we would not have become angry. Therefore, the other person made us angry. The logic is airtight. But when we think this way, a delusion is taking shape. Anger is not something that comes upon us when an offense is committed. Anger is already in us."[9]

To be clear, it is not the circumstances in our lives that make us angry. Nor is it the people around us that cause us to get angry. Anger comes from our selfish desires and pleasures. Edward Welch continues: "It's in its embryonic form, in its beginning stages, we call it desire. And this baby form is already in us in the form of our desires. We desire power, pleasure, peace, comfort, love, respect. The list could be endless. Then something stands between us and what we desire. We want something and we're not getting it. So anger is in us and it just takes the right occasion to bring it out." [10]

There are two kinds of anger mentioned in the Bible. The first is sinful anger. This is the one that Jesus and James link to murder. The second one is a righteous anger. Christ had righteous anger. We read of Him in the gospels expressing anger, but it was righteous and other-centered. When He was angry and turned over the tables in the temple, He did so to defend God's glory. We also see Him talking to the Pharisees very sternly, but again Jesus was standing for truth and God's honor and did not sin in His anger.

---

[9] Edward Welch. *Meditations on Anger, Patience, and Peace: A Small Book About A Big Problem* (Greensboro: New Growth Press, 2017), 29.

Like Jesus, we can be angry but not engage in sinful anger. This is why the apostle Paul could say, "Be angry but sin not" (See Ephesians 4:26). We do not sin when our anger is short in its duration and does not evolve into the kinds of sins expressed in Ephesians 4:31 (bitterness, evil speaking, malice, etc.).

Sinful anger is the opposite of agape love. We do not even want to flirt with it because it creates a barrier for true love to manifest in our hearts and lives. It also does something else in our relationship with God that James warns us about in his letter. James continued with his message to us in James 4 when he said:

"You adulteresses, do you not know that friendship with the world is hostility toward God? Therefore, whoever wishes to be a friend of the world makes himself an enemy of God" (James 4:4).

Essentially James is saying anger is not just a sin against man; it is ultimately a sin against God. When we indulge in sinful anger, we need to understand what is at stake: a violation of our commitment to love God and others.

James links anger to adultery. *Sinful anger is an expression* of an adulterous relationship with God. It is like a spouse having a passionate desire for someone else, instead of their spouse, and is willing to even fight others to have a relationship with this other person. God is not pleased with such adulterous behavior and calls us to repent, humble ourselves, and submit to Him, and the devil's influence over us will flee (See James 4:7-10).

It is important to note that we all have desires, most of which are natural. For example, we all have a desire for love or approval and respect. There is nothing wrong with those desires. What James is saying is when our desires have become so great that they manifest in anger, there is a great spiritual problem.

When anger is present, this is an indication that we are seeking to fulfill our desires in the wrong way. This is where spiritual adultery takes place. The most common place this happens is in our relationships. We may want approval, or love, or respect, and we are willing to fight to get it.

As disciples of Christ, we must give up our rights to have our relationships and life be the way we want it. The desires within us must be met by God. He is our source. Anything we get from our relationships with others is an overflow from what we have already received from God.

Think about a situation you may have had recently with a difficult person, which led to an argument or a fight. Perhaps you were interacting with them and just began to feel annoyed. What did you desire from the relationship or the person? Did you have a desire for that person to change? Did you believe the person was making poor decisions, and you were upset that they were not seeing your point of view?

Did you allow your anger to get the best of you because you were trying to "fix" the person or a relational issue? Listen and learn from Abraham's wife, Sarah, and avoid taking matters into your own hands.

Also, seek to have compassion and patience for the other person in a relational conflict. We do not know what their unmet desires are, and they may not even know what they are. This is the goal of agape: to live a life before others that they desire to be closer to God, love Him, and have their needs met by Him. They will not fight with us as they grow and have their desires met by God.

So how is patience connected to anger? From a Biblical perspective, the answer is very clear and simple. Patience is being slow to engage in sinful anger in response to difficult people. Specifically, biblical patience is having an emotional calm or quietness in the face of provocation. It is a calm and quietness in the face of misfortune or unfavorable circumstances. Patience never says, "I have had enough." It suffers indefinitely and continues even in the face of behavior that should really stop this love.

This quality of love is illustrated by Paul Tan (*Encyclopedia of 7700 Illustrations*). He wrote: *"that during the late 1500 s, Dr.*

Thomas Cooper edited a dictionary with the addition of 33,000 words and many other improvements. He had already been collecting materials for eight years when his wife, a rather difficult woman, went into his study one day while he was gone and burned all of his notes under the pretense of fearing that he would kill himself with study. Eight years of work – a pile of ashes! Dr. Cooper came home, saw the destruction, and asked who had done it. His wife told him boldly that she had done it. The patient man heaved a deep sigh and said, 'Oh Dinah, Dinah, thou hast given a world of trouble!' Then he quietly sat down to another eight years of hard labor to replace the notes which she had destroyed." [11]

This story illustrates beautifully this first attribute of love: patience. Sinful anger can only be defeated by love. Your aim as a Christian disciple is to make sinful anger your enemy. Sinful anger is hating others. Period. Choose not to make any excuses for your anger. There are no justifiable reasons for it.

The good news is that there is hope for all of us. We can learn to become people of patience, who are slow to anger, and loving. However, we need to lay ourselves under the divine surgeon's hands. We need to allow Him to do the surgical work in our souls to remove those things that are in us that cause us to act in ways that are unloving.

---

[11] https://www.preceptaustin.org/1corinthians_134

Remember: it is never about what is happening outside of you; it is what is happening within you. If we do not get this lesson, then we will not deal with what is inside of us, and then God's love cannot flow through us because we are blind to what is clogging up the divine love of agape that is in our hearts.

We must become people who go before our Father, the Holy Spirit, and Christ, and offer ourselves as living sacrifices. We must open up ourselves to God, and our prayer can be: *"Do what You need to do to remove sin out of my heart. Empower me to see where I am seeking to meet my desires outside of my relationship with You. Lead me, Father, on this blessed journey where You become my all-in-all and meet my needs. I desire to be a vessel of Your love to a lost and dying world. Make me into that vessel of honor that is pleasing to You. I confess that my sinful passions are an enemy to Christ's life living through me. Empower me to deny myself, take up my cross and follow You. In Jesus name I pray, amen."*

A final note: If you are in an abusive relationship and being harmed, please seek to remove yourself and your children from further danger. This is an area you need to exercise patience (agape love in general) from a safe distance.

Core Fears

Let us now turn our attention to look specifically at the desires warring within us. What if you could learn something that had more than a 90% success rate in resolving relational conflict and a 72% increase in relational satisfaction? Would you be interested?

We need to have some tools in our toolbox so that we can do our part in the process of transformation in allowing God's love to manifest through us. Our part is really dealing with presenting our sinful nature before God, identifying what is getting in the way of God's agape love, and partnering with God to change.

I want to introduce you to some research done by the late Dr. Gary Smalley. He had a 50-year career helping couples and families in being able to navigate relationships. His lessons are Bible-based and from a Christian perspective. His research detected cycles and patterns in relationships, and he learned how to break these cycles and patterns. Once they were broken, it led to relational success and healing.

Let us now discuss what Smalley called core fears. As mentioned before, we all have legitimate human desires within us. We want acceptance. We want grace. We want connection. We want honor. We want validation. We want to be understood. We want comfort, support, and approval. We want affection, etc.

Conversely, we fear rejection. We fear being misunderstood. We fear being invalidated. We fear feeling worthless. We fear being unwanted. We fear being ignored. If these desires are not being met by God, this creates relational problems when those desires go unfulfilled.

Gary Smalley wrote in his book *The DNA of Relationships:* *"Without identifying your core fear and understanding how you tend to react when your fear buttons get pushed, our relationships will suffer. Every time."* [12]

If we want to be patient – if we want to truly love – we must understand ourselves and address our core fears. We must know and understand what our triggers are. We must do our part so that our sinful nature can be dissolved by God's Spirit.

Gary Smalley also wrote: *"Most people are not aware of the fear that lurks behind many of their troubled relationships. There are two core fears that are troublesome to any relationship. They are the fear of being controlled or losing power and the fear of being disconnected, separated from people and being alone."* [13]

Here are also some core fears that Smalley identified:

"My core fear is that I feel ...
1. Helpless, powerless, impotent or controlled.

---

[12] Dr. Gary Smalley, *The DNA of Relationships* (Wheaton: Tyndale House Publishers, 2004), 42.
[13] Dr. Gary Smalley, *The DNA of Relationships* (Wheaton: Tyndale House Publishers, 2004), 42.

2. Rejected; that people are closing you out of their lives.
3. Abandoned or left behind.
4. Disconnected from others or alone.
5. Fear being a failure.
6. Unloved as if no one could love you.
7. Defective as if something is wrong with you.
8. Inadequate as if you just don't measure up like you should.
9. Don't want to feel pain emotionally or spiritually.
10. Fear of being hypocritical or phony.
11. Fear being inferior as if you were being placed before everyone else; low in value.
12. Fear being cheated or ripped off or taken advantage of.
13. Fear being invalidated as if your words or your actions are being ignored or devalued.
14. Fear being unfulfilled as if what is happening to you will lead to a dissatisfied life.
15. Fear being humiliated as if you have no dignity or self-respect.
16. Fear being manipulated as if others are deceiving you.
17. Fear isolation as if others are planning to ignore you." [14]

You can only identify your core fears through analysis (please consider reading Smalley's book to do so). Think about your relationships and the conflicts you have experienced. You will

---

[14] Dr. Gary Smalley, *The DNA of Relationships* (Wheaton: Tyndale House Publishers, 2004), 43.

realize that there was something under the surface that you feared and a desire that was within you that was unmet.

Chapter 3
The Fear Dance

Smalley also discovered another concept during his research that he labeled the fear dance. The fear dance is a pattern that starts with some relational crisis taking place. There are four components of this dance: I/You hurt, I/You Want, I/You Fear, and I/You React.

For example, someone says something to you that hurts you. The hurt feelings you now have makes you want a solution to stop how you feel.

Core fears start to come up to the surface (feelings of rejection, not being good enough, abandonment, etc.). The hurt person is now angry and vents their anger to the other person. In the exchange of angry words, the other person is hurt by what is communicated. They, too, want the hurt they feel to end due to their core fears being triggered. Now they react with angry words and actions. The other person is hurt by the other person's words, and the dance continues.

(See diagram below from *The DNA of Relationships*.)

Do you understand now how conflict can get out of control in a back and forth exchange of angry words and actions? Smalley's research confirms the truth of James 4:1-3, which identifies our desires as being the source of relational conflict.

Listen, we do not want to dance with fear. As we choose to understand what is going on within us and open the pathway for God to work within us, He will change us. As God changes us, agape can really flow through us, and our relationships will improve in time.

As you take responsibility for your own internal fears, desires, and unmet needs, your core fears will be triggered less as the Spirit gains control of you. Those triggers in you that caused you to get angry in the past will be removed, and you will instead look for solutions to relational conflicts. Indeed, you will be gradually growing into a man or a woman who is patient, slow to anger — loving.

Cultivating Patience

There is a Chinese proverb that says, *"One moment of patience may ward off great disaster. One moment of impatience may ruin a whole life."* This saying really captures the importance of patience in the life of a person – a Christian. We can destroy our entire witness just by sinful anger. So, let us make it our aim to cultivate patience.

Here are ten ways we can do so:

Number One: Bring God into the Equation.

This is the first step. God will lead you on your journey every single day. If you are looking for this attribute of love to be manifested in your life, opportunities will come daily before you. Opportunities will come today for you to exercise biblical patience, but God will be with you. Pray for the power and the filling of the Holy Spirit every day. You can pray something like this, *"God, I cannot do this without You, so I am praying that You live Your life through me to truly love others."*

Number Two: Stay Focused.

Stay focused on your ultimate goal. As disciples of Jesus Christ, our ultimate goal is to represent Christ and bring others to a true relationship with Him. Your life is a living epistle (letter) that people can read. Allow God to work in you patience and true love, so what people read of your life is agape love.

Number Three: We Need to Think Before We Speak and Act.

We need to think before we speak, particularly when someone is pushing our fear buttons. We must also do the same in regard to our actions. Ask yourself this: *"Is what I am about to say or do going to honor God, or will this do damage to His name?"*

Proverbs 15:1 says that, "A gentle answer turns away wrath." When people are acting in an unbecoming manner, if we can speak in a gentle tone, their wrath can be turned away. This is an immensely powerful way of being able to squash a spark before it becomes a blazing fire of relational conflict.

Number Four: Think Miranda Rights.

The Miranda Rights says: "You have the right to remain silent. Anything you say can or will be used against you in the court of law."

When we are going through a situation with a person, particularly a provoking situation, we need to practice silence. When someone is trying our patience, if we do not think before we speak or act, we can say things that may irrevocably change that relationship or severely damage it.

So, think Miranda when provoked – you have a right to remain silent. Choose to exercise your right to silence in the face of provocation. Remember that childhood adage, *"If you cannot say anything nice, do not say anything at all."*

One thing I have learned in my own experience is that silence in the face of provocation is a great teacher. When we choose to endure insults without responding, we gain knowledge about the person or situation that leads us to compassion and not anger. Also, we learn through silence how to not escalate an issue and destroy a person or a relationship through our words and actions. In silence, we learn wisdom. Indeed, patience and wisdom are connected.

Number Five: Forgive Quickly.

When someone has done something against you, ask God for the empowerment to let it go quickly. That is what forgiveness is all about. It is like having a pin and choosing to drop it to the ground – it is done. Do not sit and contemplate the issue repeatedly in your mind or keep a record of the wrongs done against you. When we keep rehearsing the wrongs others have done against us, forgiveness becomes almost impossible.

Number Six: Soften Your Words.

When encountering a situation that is upsetting to you, choose your words wisely. For example, suppose you are at your favorite restaurant. The server who comes to greet you is a familiar one. In the past, every time they served you, they have gotten your order wrong, which tends to get you upset and irritated. You be may be thinking, *"Oh no! Why do they always get my order wrong? I'm just so sick of them."* If you said that out loud, it would hurt the waiter. If you soften your words, first in your thoughts, you may think something like: *"It looks like they're really busy, and that is why they keep getting the order wrong."* This would lead you to have more compassion toward the server in both your words and actions. Also, we want to exercise caution in our words and tone because it encourages others around us to behave the same. So, soften your words.

Number Seven: Choose to think good things of others and put a positive construction on the activities or the actions of other people.

We live in a world where, naturally, 80% of our thoughts are negative. That means when we are thinking about people, particularly when we are in a relational conflict, we tend to think of them in negative terms. What if we changed our thinking to conform to Philippians 4:8? "Finally, brethren, whatever is true, whatever is honorable, whatever is right, whatever is pure, whatever is lovely, whatever is of good repute, if there is any excellence and if anything worthy of praise, dwell on these things."

We can pray and ask God to help us to have mercy and compassion towards others in our thought life. Our thinking can be: *"How can I bless this person through kind deeds and kind words despite how they have treated me?"* Or *"Maybe they are going through a hard time in their life and don't know how to handle it and did not mean to hurt me."* Begin to think or assume the best about the person. Love seeks to put the best possible construction on another person's actions and another person's words. Let us seek to think good things.

Number Eight: Start each day by reducing all your earthly expectations to as close to zero as possible. [15]

Gary Smalley penned those words, and they are profound. It has been said that, *"Expectations are premeditated resentment."* How true! Expectations will cause us to be resentful and angry if they go unfulfilled. We live in a fallen world, and there is always a chance that expectations will not come to pass.

---

[15] Dr. Gary Smalley, *The DNA of Relationships* (Wheaton: Tyndale House Publishers, 2004), 127.

If someone asked me, *"What is one thing that helped you to exercise Biblical patience?"* My answer would be simple: *"Reduce your expectations of that person to zero and roll all your expectations unto God."* The Spirit of God will help you.

We need to strive to not expect our life to unfold according to our will, to our timetable, and to our desires. We want to align ourselves with God's timetable and will. This should be our prayer: *"Lord, Your will be done."*

There are things that people are responsible for doing biblically, but we cannot control other people's actions. We need to stay focused on the changes that need to occur in our own lives and what we can control.

Our responsibility is to choose to love others regardless of whether they fail to meet our expectations or not. Strive to not expect life to unfold the way you think it should; reduce your expectations to zero. This will greatly reduce your stress levels.

What are the circumstances and situations that you are facing now? What are your expectations in those situations and of the people in your life?

Write your answers down and ask God to help you release all your expectations of others and life. Then choose to put all your hope in God instead.

Number Nine: Allow your emotions to be a gauge for what is going on within.

If we start to feel tension, anxiety, or anger towards a situation or person, we need to become aware of why we feel the way we do. Ask yourself questions like: "What's going on with me?" It may be something that you and God need to address. Or it might be something as simple as you are tired and need more rest.

A good way to evaluate yourself is to use the acronym H.A.L.T. Ask yourself: "Am I **H**ungry, **A**ngry, **L**onely or **T**ired?" These are four circumstances that can lead to impatience. If we know any of these conditions are present, we need to do what the acronym suggests — halt — rest.

Number Ten: Use every irritable and challenging experience as an opportunity to worship God better.

Choose to believe that every situation in your life is working for your good and is an opportunity to know Christ better. You can ask yourself, *"What are the lessons that God is seeking to teach me through this? How can this experience make me more loving?"* Indeed, this is God's goal for us: to use every opportunity to grow in agape and in Christ.

Chapter 4
Love is Kind

Kindness is universal. Everyone can recognize kindness. Biblical kindness is about doing useful deeds for someone else based on a need.

Luke 10:30-37 is a good example of kindness and mercy in action:

Jesus replied and said, "A man was going down from Jerusalem to Jericho, and fell among robbers, and they stripped him and beat him, and went away leaving him half dead. And by chance a priest was going down on that road, and when he saw him, he passed by on the other side. Likewise, a Levite also, when he came to the place and saw him, passed by on the other side. But a Samaritan, who was on a journey, came upon him; and when he saw him, he felt compassion, and came to him and bandaged up his wounds, pouring oil and wine on them; and he put him on his own beast, and brought him to an inn and took care of him. On the next day he took out two denarii and gave them to the innkeeper and said, 'Take care of him; and whatever more you spend, when I return I will repay you.' Which of these three do you think proved to be a neighbor to the man who fell into the robbers' hands?" And he said, "The one who showed mercy toward him." Then Jesus said to him, "Go and do the same."

There are several lessons we can learn about kindness from this parable.

Lesson Number One: Be kind to everyone.

Kindness is universal in that everyone can recognize its presence. As Mark Twain said, *"A language that the deaf can hear and the blind can read is kindness."*

In the parable of the Good Samaritan, Jesus tells a story about two cultural enemies and one who decided to be kind and reach out to his "enemy" in his time of need. In order to truly love, we cannot decide to be kind only to people who are kind to us or who we think deserves it.

Love knows no limits; therefore, kindness knows no limits. We also learn from this story the definition of a neighbor. Our neighbor is literally anyone who is near us – in our personal world who has a need. It could be someone who "randomly" comes across our life's path or someone who is already in our life.

Lesson Number Two: Pay attention to others.

When something looks wrong in someone's life, if you can safely do so, draw closer to the person to really observe them (physically go near or, in some cases, call or text). We see in this story that the priests and the Levite both saw the Samaritan but chose to look the other way. The Good Samaritan, on the other hand, stopped and actually got close to the person to see what was happening. When we choose to get closer to others, it gives us a good perspective as to what they really need.

Lesson Number Three: Love feels compassion.

Kindness is love's compassionate nature. Compassion is deep sympathy and sorrow for others with a strong desire to help those in need.

The Good Samaritan is a great example of compassion towards those who hate us. He demonstrates that in order to have compassion for our enemy, we need to see our common humanity. The Good Samaritan did not fill his mind with hate. He saw a human being like himself that needed help and allowed his compassion to lead him to the next lesson: action.

Lesson Number Four: True love acts.

In verses 34-35 of Luke 10, we see immediate action on the part of the Good Samaritan. Why is this important? It is important because we can see a need, we can feel compassion, but procrastinate in reaching out (or not reach out at all). The Samaritan took the man, bandaged him up, poured oil and wine on him, and put him on his own beast. He then took him to an inn. He sacrificed his time and resources to help his neighbor in need.

Showing kindness is not always convenient, but it is truly displaying agape. We must allow our lives to be "interrupted" by the needs of others and be willing to sacrifice our resources and time to help our "neighbor."

It is important to note here that kindness does involve wisdom and discernment. If we do not use wisdom and discernment in our kindness, a kind deed could seem unkind if done in the wrong context. For example, if someone lost their spouse and we give them a gift card to a restaurant and comment that, *"Hey, maybe you will find a new spouse there,"* this deed now loses its value in kindness. Our kind deed has now become "unkind." We have to be mindful of the emotional, physical, financial, social, and spiritual situations someone may be in and discern how we can best help them.

Historians believe that the story that Jesus told here was based on a common reality that was happening on the journey from Jerusalem to Jericho. It seemed that a lot of people were robbed and beaten during the journey. We do not know the reason why the Levite and the priest walked away. We can only wonder if fear played a role. The Levite and the priest could possibly have been concerned that their lives were in danger if they stopped to investigate. I think we can all relate to the natural instinct to preserve our lives.

However, the Good Samaritan had a different perspective – the perspective of true agape love. As Martin Luther King Jr. powerfully noted in his ***I've Been to the Mountaintop Speech***, *"And so the first question that the priest asked, the first question that the Levite asked was, 'If I stop to help this man, what will happen to me?'* "*But then the Good Samaritan came by, and he reversed the question: 'If I do not stop to help this man, what will happen to him?'" This is an important question we must also ask ourselves when considering displaying kindness to others ('What will happen to this person[s] today if I don't help them?').*"

True love manifests when there is more concern about others than our own lives. This, my friend, is agape. As Jesus said, "Greater love has no one than this, that one lay down his life for his friends" (John 15:13). Let us listen to the voice of God calling us to a higher level of love; a love that is willing to look beyond ourselves so that we can serve others in the spirit in which God serves and loves us.

Love is Not Envious

How do you respond to the good fortune of others? When somebody you know has a new baby, a new car, a new job –

how do you respond to those things? Are you happy for them? Are you feeling a little bit like you wish it was you? Maybe someone received a promotion over you, and you are thinking you are more qualified, and it should have been you. Are you happy when others get something spectacular? Or is watching someone celebrate their wedding anniversary a challenge to you because you are divorced?

Or what about observing people who seem to "have it all together" when your life seems to be falling apart? How do you feel? What about losing? Do you lose gracefully, or do you get upset? What is your response?

> *"If you achieve what you cannot; if they gain what you lack; if they win where you lose then the truth will come out."*
> ~ Ray Pritchard

Let us now turn our attention to that age-old green-eyed monster called envy. We have talked about love being patient and kind, which has been mentioned before as positive attributes of love. Paul now lists eight negatives that help us to see what love is not. Envy is the first one.

I have asked you many questions earlier. I did so because if I asked you, *"Do you envy others?"* your immediate response may be, *"No, I'm not that kind of person. I don't have that in me."* Envy is something that can pop up unaware in our journey in the Christian life. We all possess a sinful nature, and our hearts are prone to deceit, so be careful in being quick to say that envy has no place in your heart.

The degree to which envy is present may vary from person to person, based on Christ's work in us. Our ability to love is compromised when the negatives are there, and we cannot love others in the way that God has called us to love.

The negatives of love are circumstantial. In other words, we may not know we have them unless we are placed in the right circumstances for them to come out. And when they do, we must present them before God and ask Him to help us to be cleansed of these things so that true agape can flow through us.

Let us turn our attention to the word envy. Some Bible translations use the word "jealous" instead of "envy." What is the difference? Envy is wanting what someone else has. Jealousy is about holding on to what you already have. The word "envy" comes from a word that really means boiling over. It means you are striving for something, or you are burning over with some deep emotion inside of you. This deep emotion that is boiling over in you desires something that someone else has.

Envy can manifest in two ways. The first form of envy is desiring someone's possessions, lifestyle, relationships, or character. The second form is not so much about desiring someone or something someone has, but not wanting someone to have what they have (even if you don't want it). This form of envy can be compared to a child with many toys, but when they see their sibling start playing with one of their toys, they become envious. The child who is envious will leave all their other toys and demand that their sibling gives them "their" toy even though they do not need it.

There are many examples of envy in the Word of God. Remember the stories of David and Saul, and Joseph and his brothers. Envy is at the heart of each of those stories. The best example of envy is found in Genesis in the story of Cain and Abel.

We read in Genesis 4:1-8, "Now the man had relations with his wife Eve, and she conceived and gave birth to Cain, and she said, "I have gotten a manchild with the help of the Lord." Again, she gave birth to his brother Abel. And Abel was a keeper of flocks, but Cain was a tiller of the ground. So it came about in the course of time that Cain brought an offering to the Lord of the fruit of the ground. Abel, on his part also brought of the firstlings of his flock and of their fat portions. And the Lord had regard for Abel and for his offering; but for Cain and for his offering He had no regard. So Cain became very angry and his countenance fell. Then the Lord said to Cain, "Why are you angry? And why has your countenance fallen? If you do well, will not your countenance be lifted up? And if you do not do well, sin is crouching at the door; and its desire is for you, but you must master it." Cain told Abel his brother. And it came about when they were in the field, that Cain rose up against Abel his brother and killed him."

Can you see from Cain and Abel's story how envy is antithetical to love? Cain was probably thinking, *"You shouldn't have been accepted by God. I should have been accepted."* Cain's envy caused anger, and anger led to murder. Love cannot exist where envy exists. Agape love cannot exist in an environment where it is self-centered and all about us.

Envy, left unchecked, leads to hatred and resentment. This hatred could lead to the harm of someone (physically or through words). This is worth repeating: sinful anger must become our enemy if we are to become people who agape love can flow through.

These are steps we can take to combat envy in our hearts:

Step One: Go before God.

When envy rises within us, we must bring it before God and ask for His forgiveness and the cleansing of this sin.

Step Two: We need to seek to please God.

Abel pleased God – Cain did not. A simple solution for Cain would have been a prayer: *"God, what is it that You're looking for? My first offering was rejected by You, but what are You looking for?"*

When we see other people being blessed, we simply can inquire as to what they are doing and do the same thing. Success leaves clues. Let us not move to envy. Instead, get close to that person in a loving way and ask questions. *"How did you accomplish this?" "How did you get to this place?"* Follow the guidance that you are given and daily seek to honor God in all you do. As we do that, those blessings will also be in our lives.

Step Three: Practice gratitude.

Envy does not live in a grateful heart. Thank God for everything He has done for you. Look for the ways in which He has worked in your life and blessed you. Daily, seek new opportunities to say, *"Thank you, God."*

Step Four: Do not compare.

It has been said that *"Comparison is the thief of joy."* So true! Comparison will steal our joy and lead us to a place of envy. If we are so focused on what other people have and we are comparing ourselves, constant envy is inevitable. The Word of God cautions us not to do this.

You are unique, and your life's circumstances are unique. Choose not to believe that the grass is greener on their side of the fence. Cultivate your own garden (life) and be grateful. God can bless you where you are, so bloom where you are planted.

Step Five: Celebrate the success of others.

When people do great things, celebrate with them. Cain could have taken a different approach when his sacrifice was rejected. He could have chosen to learn something from his brother. We need to stop viewing life as a competition. Life is not a competition. We all win when we are in Christ Jesus.

Step Six: Be generous.

Let us strive to share with others. We must become a people of magnanimous generosity. As we share with others and we are not concerned about the spotlight being on us, envy will flee. Our concern for others will lead us to ask questions such as, *"How can I shine the light on others? How can I help others? How can I support others?"*

Chapter 5
Love is Not Arrogant

Have you ever heard someone say or found yourself saying, *"Oh, I don't need to learn about that because I know that already?"* Or *"I'm loyal, I'm committed. You're not going to find anyone as loyal and as committed as I am."* Or *"I don't associate with people like that."* This is arrogance. You may think you are not arrogant, but I caution you not to be so quick to say you are not. We all struggle with sin, and pride is at the heart of every sin.

Love is not arrogant. Arrogance is being puffed up – seeing oneself as more important and more valuable than others. Love does not have an inflated sense of itself.

Love also does not brag. What does it mean to brag? Bragging is ultimately praising yourself and your accomplishments. Love does not seek the spotlight. It is comfortable being behind the scenes.

While we are to have a godly understanding of our worth and our value, arrogance has an *overinflated* view of oneself – and that is the difference. God hates pride, and love cannot flourish in an atmosphere of arrogance and pride.

We cause harm in our relationships when arrogance is present. When we are arrogant, we cannot see the value and worth of other people in our lives. For instance, if a husband believes that he is the hardest worker in the family, and no one works as hard as he does, how can he see the contributions of his wife to their lives? If that husband cannot see the work and contributions his wife brings to their family, he will lack an appreciation for all she is and all she does. Do you get the point? If we cannot see the other person clearly, how can we truly love them? Simply put, pride destroys our ability to love others.

Additionally, when arrogance is present in a person, they see their beliefs and actions as the standard for living. Arrogance is about having life and relationships go "my way." When we are arrogant, we will seek to control and manipulate others to conform to the way we envision life. The reality is, we do not have the right to make anyone conform to what we believe or desire. Not even God forces us to do what He knows is right. We should follow in His footsteps.

So, how do we begin to get rid of this hugely inflated "I" in our lives? Here are some steps to follow:

Step One: Ask God to help you daily see your arrogance.

God will show you where arrogance shows up in your life. Let me tell you, what He shows you may shock you. You will bow your knee to Him realizing that the beast of arrogance and pride lies within all of us. Only God can show it to us. We cannot see it in ourselves.

Do not be discouraged. We serve a great God who is able to not only show us ourselves but change us. It may sometimes hurt when God gives us a little scourge, but the healing touch always follows. It is always for our good. God is not going to show you something and leave you battered and bruised on the side. He never does that. He will transform you.

Step Two: Rely on God

Begin each day bringing your soul before God and asking Him to reveal any form of arrogance in your life. As He reveals areas of arrogance, confess and repent of it. Ask God to cleanse you from all unrighteousness. Trust that He is faithful to do this. Let the cross of Jesus Christ crucify these areas of your life so that you die, and Christ lives out His humble life through you.

Arrogance can only live in a heart that compares oneself to others and not to God. You can begin this journey of change by reading the entirety of Isaiah 40 and studying it daily until your heart is filled with God's glory and is bathed in humility.

Also, ask God to reveal more of who He is to you. The goal is to get a proper appraisal of God, ourselves, and others. As the apostle Paul stated, "For through the grace given to me I say to everyone among you not to think more highly of himself than he ought to think; but to think so as to have sound judgment, as God has allotted to each a measure of faith" (Romans 12:3). Relying on God's power will change us and give us the sound judgment we need to love others the agape way.

Lastly, pray daily that Christ's presence increases in your life, and you decrease. God will allow situations in your life to humble you so His love can truly flow through you.

Step Three: Pray to be rooted in the love of God.

God desires that His love would be so strong that the praises and the good opinions of people will not enter our spirit in a way that causes pride. It is only the praise and commendation of God that truly matters.

When we root ourselves in the love of God, we do not need to prove ourselves to anyone, feel superior over anyone, fear the disapproval of others, or hurt others to feel better about ourselves.

Love is Not Rude

Do you give someone your undivided attention when they are talking to you? Do you hide behind sarcasm to get your point across? Do you interrupt people when they are talking? This is rude behavior, although we have normalized it as a society. However, love is not rude.

When the Word of God speaks of rudeness, it is basically referring to good manners – a pattern of decency. It is bad manners to not give your undivided attention when someone is talking. It is rude to put someone down using sarcasm. It is rude to interrupt people when they are talking.

When we are being rude, we really are not thinking about how our actions are affecting another person (it comes back to self-centeredness). However, if you truly care about someone, you will think about them in what you say and do.

Pastor Steven J. Cole, of Flagstaff Christian Fellowship in Arizona, tells a story about a husband who was married for many years and never opened the car door for his wife. The man's wife died, and the funeral director asked him to open up the car door of the hearse for his wife. The husband stood by the car door and paused for a little while. He realized that his wife's funeral was the first and the last time he ever opened the door for her. We simply cannot love others fully when we lack basic manners and decency.

A helpful way to evaluate whether our behavior is rude or not is to apply the Golden Rule. In other words, ask yourself, *"Would I like someone to do or say this to me?"*

Here are some other ways to address this issue:

Step One: Pray for the Holy Spirit to reveal areas in your life where you are being rude.

We need to pray for God's grace in our lives to not be rude. Without God's grace and love, we have a natural bend toward rudeness. Seek God and ask Him, "What are the right behaviors in this situation? Please help me to do it." Pray for Him to search your heart and reveal to you how you tend to be rude toward others.

Step Two: Surrender yourself daily to Him.

There is a divine surgery that God wants to do on our hearts so that we can reflect Him in the earth. We can change. God knows where you are when it comes to agape love. His desire is to grow this fruit of love: the crown jewel of the Christian faith, in each of us — in you. He will use everyday situations in your life to help you to practice being a person of good manners. Pray for the ability to see when God is calling you to be a person of decency and good manners in ordinary, everyday life experiences. He will show you.

Step Three: Get in the Word.

We need to study the Word of God to see what He says about rudeness and love. As we reflect and marinate on God's Word, His Spirit will renew our perspectives on what we previously considered good behavior but was actually rude behavior. God's Word is key in the transformation process to truly becoming a person of love.

Step Four: Honor the presence of others in your midst.

In our busy world, we struggle to really acknowledge and connect with others because of our hurried lifestyle. When someone comes into your presence, practice acknowledging them. A simple smile will go a long way. Every person that God has made is important to Him, and therefore they should be important to us.

People often feel unseen and unloved, and a seemingly simple act like acknowledging someone's presence can make them feel seen, valued, and loved.

Step Five: Become a good listener.

Good listeners are hard to find. Let us strive to become better listeners. When someone is talking to you, stop what you are doing and focus on them and what they are communicating. Seek to practice looking the person directly in their eyes and confirm what they are saying by occasionally making statements like, *"Is this what you are saying? Do I understand correctly that this is what you mean?"*

I recommend reading Robert Bolton's book *People Skills*. It is an excellent resource in helping us to understand good communication skills and how to become better listeners. This is important because when we become better listeners, we can make people feel understood. When people feel understood, they feel loved.

Step Six: Learn to wait.

Patience is a quality of love, as we already discussed, and impatience can lead to rudeness. For instance, say we are standing in a line at the bank, and it is moving slowly. We may begin to express our frustration to others in a disrespectful and rude way.

Instead of being rude and disrespectful to anyone, find something productive to do while you wait. Maybe you can read some edifying material on your phone. Perhaps you can return some email messages or connect to some people via text.

By the way, you may not want to be talking on your phone as you could disturb those who are also waiting in the line (this would be rude).

Step Seven: Choose your words wisely when you speak.

For this step, you can use what is called the sandwich method. The sandwich method is used when we have something difficult to communicate with someone. We start with a positive comment that is true about that person. Afterward, you can move to what you see needs correcting. Then end with a positive comment about the person. Here is an example: A wife and husband are living together, and the husband always leaves his stuff all over the house. The wife could say to the husband, *"I'm so glad that you are so kind and loving. You know what would really help me is if you could pick up some of the clothes that you have on the floor. That would really be of great service to me if you could do that. I am so grateful for you. I'm thankful that you are not just comfortable with our home, but comfortable with me and that our life together is the way that it is."*

Do you see the method in action now? Simply sandwich your correction with two positives at the beginning and the end of what you have to say. When reflecting upon what you will say, practice the Golden Rule: communicate in a way that you would want others to communicate with you.

Chapter 6
Love is Humble

While it is our duty to worship God, our human tendency is to worship ourselves. God's desire is for us to no longer be self-centered and focused on honoring and glorifying ourselves, but to honor and glorify *Him*.

When God is at the center, it changes how we think and behave towards people. Truly loving people means we respect their point of view and their ways of living. Love does not insist on its own way, and it is not irritable when people or life does not conform to its expectations.

Love is humble. All the negatives of love (love is not arrogant, does not boast, not self-seeking, etc.) reveals the vital connection between love and humility. One cannot exist without the other. We simply cannot grow in our life with God without humility – without the ability to see our true selves in light of His perfect life. Without humility, we can live in deception and believe that we are masters of Christian virtues like love and cannot see daily our need for God's grace to grow into the image of His Son.

Many of us perhaps have heard numerous sermons on love. We can easily stand before God's holy Word and hear the checklist of Christian love in 1 Corinthians 13:4-8 and say "Check. Yes, I am patient." Next attribute, kindness, "Check. I am kind. I serve people all the time." Love bears all things and always protects the reputation of others. "Yes, that is me." Love believes the best about others, "Check. I am, too." Next attribute, love hopes all things. "Check. I hope the best for all people in my life." Final attribute: love endures all the things. "Check. I don't give up on others easily." This is a picture of a prideful response to God's Word (you may have great growth in your life in these attributes — but none of us will ever arrive in being without sin while on earth). Christlikeness and becoming vessels of agape cannot occur with those who lack humility (See James 4:6).

We need the light of the Holy Spirit to see where we fail to love others in the way God requires. Once we see how we are not loving others, we can pray. We can pray, *God, how impatient I can be with my spouse and my children, have mercy on me."* Or *Father, I am so quick to share the shortcomings of my spouse with my friends. Empower me, through Your Spirit, to love my spouse by protecting his/her reputation."* Or "God, I am often doubtful of people s intentions and seem to be so ready to assume the worst about others. Have mercy; I need Your grace."

Listen: only the grace of God can meet our need to love as He loves, and His grace comes only through humility. Love, like many other Christian virtues, is a journey – a process of maturity, a journey of a lifetime. None of us ever arrives on this side of eternity. If we feel confident that we have arrived, I seriously question that belief. In fact, humility is lacking when we believe that we have arrived in full maturity in all attributes of love (See 1 Corinthians 13:4-8).

We must all be able to stand before the perfect mirror of God's Word in 1 Corinthians 13 and ask for the light of the Holy Spirit to reveal our own hearts and lives when compared to the life of Christ. God's grace is sufficient, and His power is made perfect in our weakness.

Here are some principles that we can follow to allow God to transform us into more humble people:

Step One: Pray daily to be filled with the Spirit of God.

Pray that Jesus will give us His humility so we can live His humble life through us.

Step Two: Accept every humiliation.

Accept every insult, every nasty word, every offense that happens to you every day. Let your response be, *"Thank You, Lord, for this humiliation."* It is not going to feel good, but it is needed to knock down the self-centered person that lives within us, so that the risen Christ can rise within us.

Step Three: Feast on God's Word daily.

Pay close attention to the life of Christ in the gospels. Study His actions and take note of His humble acts. He is the ultimate example of humility.

Step Four: Embrace truth, even if a lie would save you.

Even when the truth hurts, embrace it. If it is true about you, bring it to God.

Step Five: Become teachable.

A man or woman of humility is open to truth. They are teachable and listen to others. Arrogant people do not listen and are not willing to consider other points of view. God wants us to be people who are open so that when He speaks truth to us, we hear, we respond, and we obey. Be willing to listen to others, even when you may not respect the person. A closed mind is the end of discipleship. When we are teachable, we open ourselves up to true discipleship and growth in agape and Christlikeness.

Love Has Amnesia

Why does love have a poor memory? This is simply because love does not keep a record of wrongs. The term "record" is an accounting term. It is referring to entries placed into a ledger, which must be detailed and accurate.

In a typical accounting ledger, there are two columns: one for debits and the other for credits. When we choose not to forgive someone, we have chosen to keep detailed records that lead to an overwhelming number of debits (the negative things) held against those who wrong us. The problem here is that we are not focusing on the credits (the positive things), which would create a more favorable accounting of that person.

So, I ask you: when someone has wronged you, do you get historical? In other words, do you bring up all they have done against you in the past? Love does not keep detailed and accurate entries in our hearts about the wrongs done against us.

Warren Wiersbe said he once knew a man who actually, *"kept a written list of the rotten things people had done to him. He also said that man was one of the most miserable people he had ever known. Many people keep mental lists of the slights they have suffered. They never get over what happened in the past. They dwell on it, they live in it, they ferment in it, and as a result, they let the past shape their present and their future."*[16]

---

[16] http://www.keepbelieving.com/sermon/why-love-has-a-bad-memory/

If we keep a record of wrongs, we make ourselves miserable like the guy in Warren Wiersbe's story. Love needs to have a poor memory because if we dwell on the wrongs that others have done against us, this often leads to resentment, bitterness, hatred, slander, malice, and an unhappy life. Love is quick to hit the delete button in a relationship. Love is always ready to say, *"Oh, that was in the past. I'm done with that."*

If agape is to flow through us, then we must become people who remember wrongs done against us but choose to forgive. It is difficult for human beings to forget. However, not holding the offense against someone is supernatural. God will give us the grace to do this as we pray for it.

Let us allow the Spirit of God to remove all that we have filed in the bitterness department in our hearts. The Psalmist said in Psalm 51:10, "Create in me a clean heart, O God, and renew a steadfast spirit within me." This must be the prayer of our hearts.

Here are four practical applications in beginning the journey of not keeping records of wrongs.

Application One: Pray the Scriptures.

We can choose specific Scriptures that deal with forgiveness as an object of study and prayer. As we pray Scripture back to

God, He will empower us to release the bitterness that is in our hearts.

Application Two: Expect imperfections in our relationships and prepare to extend grace.

The reality is that in all our relationships, we are dealing with imperfect people. We experience great disappointment if we have high expectations of people, rather than rolling those expectations onto God.

Application Three: Forgive quickly.

Jesus talks about the necessity to love and to forgive others as God (in Christ) has forgiven us. God forgives us quickly and separates our sin from us as far as the East is from the West. God chooses not to bring back up our sins or hold them against us.

Application Four: Change your thinking.

The people who have wronged us also have good qualities about them. We want to focus on those good things they have done (and the good aspects of their character) rather than on the wrongs they have done (See Philippians 4:8).

Chapter 7
Love Rejoices with the Truth

We live in a world that loves to revel in gossip, rumors, or the sinful behaviors of others. However, love rejoices with truth. Love rejoices when good things happen when truth wins out over evil and lies. Agape is a kind of love that loves to respond with good to evil and rejoices in seeing the right thing done.

In 2 Samuel 1:11-16, we read about David and his love for doing the right thing.

"Then David took hold of his clothes and tore them, and so also did all the men who were with him. They mourned and wept and fasted until evening for Saul and his son Jonathan and for the people of the Lord and the house of Israel, because they had fallen by the sword. David said to the young man who told him, "Where are you from?" And he answered, "I am the son of an alien, an Amalekite." Then David said to him, "How is it you were not afraid to stretch out your hand to destroy the Lord's anointed?" And David called one of the young men and said,

"Go, cut him down." So he struck him and he died. David said to him, "Your blood is on your head, for your mouth has testified against you, saying, 'I have killed the Lord's anointed.'"

Jonathan was the son of Saul and the best friend of David. David loved him. David found out that both Jonathan and his father, Saul, had died. Saul hated David and did not show any qualities of love for David.

David mourned the loss of King Saul and Jonathan. He did not rejoice as he took no pleasure in Saul's death. David recognized that Saul was a man that had been chosen by God. He respected Saul's position even though he had terrorized him. David's compassion is also evident here. David regarded the loss of human life as something to be mourned and not to revel in.

The natural human heart would not have responded as David did. King David had the Spirit of God upon his life. He showed that a man or woman of God does not rejoice when evil or bad things happen, even to one's enemy.

In Matthew 5:48, Jesus teaches about being perfect as our heavenly Father is perfect. In this context, perfection is seen as loving one's enemy – loving those who are not living in truth and righteousness.

No matter how evil someone is, God still loves them. God is good towards all people, irrespective of whether they love and serve Him. He wants His children to model the same loving behavior in the world. The ultimate goal of Christian maturity is to love everyone, even our enemies or the enemies of God.

Here are four steps in allowing God to empower us to love in this way:

Step One: Ask daily for empowerment.

Choose not to rejoice when bad things happen to people who do not like you. We need God's perspective of people so we can see them as He sees them. This will help balance the scales, so we realize that we are not morally superior over anyone.

We are all sinners saved by grace, and we need not gloat over the sins or lies that are in someone else's life.

Step Two: Create a prayer list.

Keep a running list where you can pray for people who are not living their lives well (whether you hear about them on the news or you know them personally).

Develop the habit of praying and asking God to bless that person[s] with His presence, love, grace, and His wisdom.

Step Three: Refuse to listen to gossip.

When people want to tell you some "juicy" gossip, refrain from listening. Stop them in their tracks. Kindly and lovingly decline to hear it. You may look a little bit smug and self-righteous, but you can just say to them, *"Can we talk about something else?"* If they insist, then excuse yourself and leave their presence.

Step Four: Celebrate others.

When you notice people making positive changes in their lives, choose to compliment them. For instance, if someone is struggling with an addiction and are making changes and embracing truth in their lives, celebrate their wins with them.

Love and Service

When most Christians speak about love, they tend to focus on the service aspect of love: kindness. While at the heart of agape love is sacrificial service to others, agape love is not merely about doing kind deeds. We can have a false sense of our walk in love if we limit love to simply serving others and being kind.

What distinguishes Christian love more than any other world religion is the inspired definition given by the apostle Paul in verses 4-8 of 1 Corinthians 13. Imagine with me an orange. If we were to give someone an orange that had several segments taken out of it, immediately they would know that parts of the orange were missing. The orange is incomplete. The same is true with love. If we define Christian love merely by sacrificial acts of service, it is like giving someone an orange with missing segments. Love is simply incomplete without ALL the attributes of it.

Think with me for a moment about a wife who is exemplary in her service to her husband and family. She is consistent in taking care of all the needs of her household. She washes the family's clothes, cleans the home, prepares the meals, pays the bills, supports her husband and children in all their daily activities (love is kind). But this wife has a short fuse (love is patient). It doesn't take much to get her angry, and when she gets angry, everyone will know about it. She shares with her closest friends the shortcomings, mistakes, and the poor decisions of her husband (love protects). She believes that the shortcomings in her husband will never change (love hopes all things), and she makes him know that she really does not believe in him (love believes all things). Her children can sense that their mom is always quick to believe the worst about them and that they will make bad decisions (love believes all things). And when her husband and children make choices that displease her, she wishes for a divorce (love endures all things). Her children and husband have come to believe that they are a burden. Although this mom and wife serves her family selflessly, she lacks true agape love in its fullness.

Here, my friend, we see the challenge of a shallow and narrow view of love. Although this wife is sacrificial and does many kind deeds, her family may feel completely unloved, and they would be right.

Paul underscores this point before introducing a complete definition of biblical love (See 1 Corinthians 13:4-8). In the first three verses of 1 Corinthians 13:1-3, Paul makes clear that sacrificial acts ALONE is not a complete definition of love. The Apostle Paul is essentially saying, *"Oh, you are using your gifts, that is great, but don't boast in that. Do you truly love others? I want you to see true love in what I am about to say in verses 4-8."* There are other aspects of love that must be taken into account when evaluating our journey to love. Indeed, agape love is the crown jewel of the Christian faith, and like any jewel, there are many facets of that jewel that makes it what it is.

So sure, we can sacrifice all we can for others, but if we lack patience (we have a short fuse and get angry with the faults of others easily), or lack the power to believe the best about others, feel hopeless about them, fail to protect their reputation in our interactions with others, or are willing to give up easily on them, then our love is incomplete and we must still mature in true biblical love.

Chapter 8
Love Bears All Things

When you hear some bad news about someone, are you a talebearer who is anxious to go and tell others what you just heard? Or when talking to someone about a difficult person in your life, do you exercise judgment in what you share to protect that person's reputation?

Love bears all things. The word "bear" refers to a covering — like a roof covering on a building. In other words, love covers or conceals the sins of others. It has been translated this way: "Love is slow to expose." This phrase really captures the meaning of love bearing all things.

In essence, love throws a cloak of silence over what is not pleasing in another person. The reality is that love does not broadcast another person's problems (privately or publicly). Ultimately, love is slow to expose the weaknesses of other people to protect their reputation – "Love protects."

One theologian said this: "Love will not lie about people's weaknesses or protect sin, but it protects others from the exposure to ridicule, or harm." It is not showing ignorance to other people's weaknesses but being slow to expose it to others to protect someone's reputation from harm.

Now there are occasions where we must expose something that is harmful to others. In our revealing of the truth, we can still take steps to protect the person[s] reputation to the best of our ability. John Wesley said, *"Whatever evil the Lover of mankind sees, hears or knows of anyone, He mentions it to none. It never goes out of the Creator's lips unless where absolute duty constraints to speak."* Let us strive to do the same.

Here are some illustrations for you to consider:

Illustration One:

If someone anxiously comes up to you and says they have something to tell you about one of your church sisters/brothers, refuse to listen. Love protects.

Illustration Two:

If your spouse has a pattern of behavior that irritates you, do not jump on the phone and go tell a family member or friend. Remember, love protects. If you share it, harm will come to the reputation of your spouse.

By irritation, I am not speaking of abuse. If you are being abused, please seek help and get to a safe place.

Illustration Three:

You just heard a news report on T.V. about some government officials you do not like. You decide to post on Facebook insulting remarks about these officials. Remember, love protects. Choose to pray for those politicians. God has the power to help you walk as a child of light – to walk in love.

Here are some necessary steps in the process:

Step One: Repent.

We want to repent for being the CNN of other people's lives by broadcasting their problems. Go to God in prayer. Ask Him for forgiveness for all the times [knowingly and unknowingly] you did not protect the reputation of others. Pray for the power to turn from this sin to truly love others.

Step Two: Ask to be filled with His Spirit.

We need God to make the right choices and to love in general. If this has been a pattern in your life, pray for grace in the moments of temptation.

Step Three: Practice focusing on and speaking well of others.

This is especially important. We must practice looking for the good in others so that we can speak well of them. When we focus on people's sins it makes it easier to gossip and ruin the reputation of others.

Step Four: Refuse to listen to gossip.

When people come to you with gossip, refuse to listen to it. Choose to literally walk away from gossip.

Step Five: Protect the reputation of others at all costs.

Make a conscious decision to protect the reputation of other people by not sharing bad information about them. In other words, do not spread gossip. We must be slow to expose unless duty constrains us to expose what is happening in someone else's life.

Love Believes All Things

Love believes all things ultimately refers to trust and faith. Love trusts and has faith in God and others. To love God is to believe in Him, and His promises completely. It is to trust that God will always work all things in our life for our good.

In regard to our relationships with others, love is not suspicious. Love gives people the benefit of the doubt and chooses to believe the best about others and not the worst.

Let me share a story about Thomas Edison that may best illustrate this point. We now know Thomas as the inventor of the light bulb. However, when Thomas was in school, he was a poor student. He was described by his teachers as "addled" or unable to think clearly.

However, Edison had a mom who believed all things. She believed in her son. His mother's faith in him paved the way for his belief in his own potential. Who knows if the light bulb would have ever been invented if it was not for a mom whose love believed all things. Edison once said, *"My mother was the making of me. She was so sure of me, and I felt I had someone to live for, someone I must not disappoint."* Wow! This is the power of love believing all things.

Now believing the best about others does not mean we do not see their deficiencies. It is just that we choose to focus on the best about the person. We clearly see the things that are wrong, but we choose not to focus on them.

When God looks at each of us, He sees the best. He sees what His grace can produce in us in spite of our sinful tendencies. God chooses to use people that we probably would not choose.

Would you have used murderers to accomplish a task for you? Well, God did. Moses, Paul, and David all committed murder. Yet God chose each of them to accomplish His purposes. Why? Because love believes all things.

But what if we believe in someone and our worst fears are confirmed? This is where love hopes all things comes into play. We will talk about that in the next chapter.

Here are some ways we can partner with God to be a vessel of agape's quality of believing all things:

Step One: Build your trust in God-muscles.

Make it your aim to read God's Word daily. God's Word builds our trust-muscle. As we daily study and meditate on the Word of God, He strengthens our faith.

Step Two: Become a trustworthy person.

God is trustworthy and faithful, and we, as His people, should mirror these qualities in our own lives. If we are not trustworthy, this creates a barrier for others to believe in the God we say we serve.

If you say you are going to do something, do it. Do not say one thing and do something else. We must be consistent in our words and deeds. Otherwise, people will lose trust in us, and they will not believe anything we say.

If you lose your influence on someone, you cannot speak into their lives because they do not see you as a credible person.

Step Three: Be a balcony person.

The term "balcony people" comes from the book *Balcony People* by Joyce Heatherly. She differentiates between two kinds of people. There are "balcony people," and there are "basement people." Basement people are often critical of others and tear people down.

On the other hand, "balcony people" affirm others. They encourage other people and lift them up. We all have the power, through the love of God, to make someone's day by saying or doing something to help them to know that someone believes in them.

Step Four: Choose to put the best possible meaning on other people's actions and words.

No matter how a situation looks, seek to assume the best about the person who is involved in that situation. Practice taking your worst assumptions about someone and putting a good meaning in its place.

Chapter 9
Love Hopes All Things

Have you ever gone through an experience where you were so downtrodden, your heart was so broken, you were in so much despair, and then someone said something to you, and suddenly your soul brightened up, and you felt better?

Love hopes all things. Hope, my friend, is immensely powerful. Hope is something that we can easily forget about as an attribute of love. Hope is often that neglected part of our spiritual lives, but it is so important. If we love someone, but feel hopeless about them and their situation, we really do not love them completely.

Biblical hope is godly optimism. Hope holds on to the possibility that brighter days are ahead – that life and people can change for the better. Biblical hope means we are looking forward to something with confidence. Hope is an expression or a desire for some good with the expectation of obtaining it.

We place our hope in so many things. We can put our hope in people, our circumstances, money, our careers, in anything. However, we misplace our hope if we place it in anything or anyone other than God. When we put our hope in God, we are trusting that He will bring about the best possible outcome in regard to a situation or person[s]. While sometimes we may not get the outcome we expect, we are guaranteed that our hopes are not misplaced when we put them in God. He knows what is best and will always do what is the greatest good for us.

Pastor John MacArthur of the Grace Community Church in Sun Valley California, once told this story about a dog. The dog lived in an airport in a large city for over five years. He was waiting for his master to return after losing him in the airport. Employees and other people fed the dog, and they took care of him. However, the dog would not leave the spot where he last saw his master. This dog would not give up hope that someday his master would return, and they would be reunited. If a dog can have such a love for his master that can produce this kind of hope, how much more should we, as children of God, cultivate hope? We have a greater capacity than a dog to "hope against hope" like Abraham (See Romans 4:18), even when it looks foolish to others. Love will not despair and instead will say, "God is able!"

Through hope, particularly hope in God, we can recover from anything. We can survive any situation with hope. Many survivors of the Nazi concentration camps and those who have experienced unspeakable abuse and tragedy attribute hope to their ability to survive.

Norman Cousins shared the story of Dr. William Buchholz in the *Western Journal of Medicine*. Buchholz says that he overheard two oncologists talking about papers that they were going to present at an American Society of clinical oncology meeting. One of the doctors was complaining about the results he received with his lung cancer patients compared with the other doctor and his patients. He was confused about why they were getting different results when they both were giving the same drugs, dosage, entry criteria, and schedule.

The doctor who was complaining got a 22% response rate while the other got a rate of 74%. The complaining doctor asked the other doctor, *"How do you do it?"*

The other doctor said that while they were using the same drugs, he gave his patients HOPE and told them that they had a chance. Hope was responsible for a miraculous response rate for the treatment of lung cancer. Hope is that powerful. [17]

Here are some steps we can follow to apply these truths to our lives:

---

[17] Norman Cousins. *Head First, The Biology of Hope.* New York: E. P. Dutton, 1989, 99.

Step Number One: Focus on God's promises.

When you are feeling hopeless, put your hope in God by focusing on His promises (See Psalm 62:5). Go to God's Word and find Scriptures that inspire hope. A great promise you can start with is Isaiah 40:31. It says: "But those who wait on the Lord shall renew their strength; they shall mount up with wings like eagles, they shall run and not be weary, they shall walk and not faint." (NKJV).

Step Number Two: Keep connected.

Stay connected to God through prayer. If something is of special concern to you, keep going to God about that situation. God can and will intercede on your behalf and those you love.

Step Number Three: Expect good things.

In whatever we face, be confident that God can do more than you dare ask or think. Meditate on Scripture like Ephesians 3:20, which says: "Now to Him who is able to do exceedingly abundantly above all that we ask or think, according to the power that works in us." Put a hopeful spin on your situation. For example, instead of thinking someone will never change, believe that God is in the midst of the situation and will do what is best.

Regardless of what the situation looks like, God has the power to change it. Trust that God can do all things and wait in expectation, in hope, for what He is going to do.

Step Number Four: Speak life about others.

When we speak negatively about people and about a situation, we are speaking death. This does not inspire hope. Speak life about others, and this will build hope.

Step Number Five: Review God's resume.

Go back and think about what God has done in the past. Review His resume in your life; let that build your hope. If God has helped you in the past, surely He will help you in the present and the future.

Hold on to hope because we know we serve a God who is mighty, great, and powerful.

Step Number Six: Get inspired.

Seek out people who have been in your shoes and listen to their stories and how they endured. Find books or videos of people who have been in similar situations that inspire hope in your heart.

Step Number Seven: Put your future into perspective.

Your today does not have to determine your tomorrow. Tomorrow could be better because we serve a powerful God. Trust your unknown future to the God you know is capable of changing anything.

Step Number Eight: Encourage someone.

When we encourage others, it fills our own soul with hope. So, the next time you are feeling hopeless, find someone you know that is going through a difficult time, and bring joy into their world. We are always blessed when we focus on others rather than ourselves.

Step Number Nine: Tap into your hope team.

Your hope team are those people who cheer you on and inspire you the most when you are feeling down. Call these people. Ask them to pray for you or to give you a word of encouragement. When you are feeling hopeless, do not isolate yourself, and attempt to handle the situation alone. This is the time to reach out to your hope team and partner with others on your journey.

Love Endures All Things

What do you do when you have protected someone's reputation after they have wronged you? What do you do when you believed the best about someone repeatedly, and your worse fears are confirmed? What do you do when you hoped they would change, and things would be different, but nothing changes? This is where love endures all things comes in.

What does endure really mean? Endure comes from a Greek word that means to abide under or to stay. To love someone is to abide or stay under challenging circumstances (except abuse). Love continues to suffer with the grievances of others, despite its difficulty.

Love does not give up easily. Love never gives up on people, no matter what they do. Love's capacity for suffering is big. When thinking about enduring all things in your relationships, reflect upon God's capacity to love us in spite of our sinful patterns and hurtful behavior.

Here are some steps to help you to endure:

Step One: Seek the divine Counselor.

Whatever situation we face in life, God can counsel us. Tell God about the situation you are facing. Ask Him for wisdom (See James 1:5-8). When you are faced with a troubled relationship, pray this prayer: *"God, I love You. I want to do what's right. I don't know what to do. Please give me wisdom. What can I do in this relationship? Please help me to be able to endure in this relationship and do what pleases you."*

Step Two: Claim God's promises and cast your cares on Him.

When faced with a challenging relationship, search God's Word for relevant Scriptures that address your situation. God can show you Scriptures that are relevant to your situation. Claim the promises of God and have faith He will fulfill them.

Cast your cares on the Lord as you wait for Him to fulfill His promises. Each time this difficult relationship feels like a burden, just keep casting it onto the Lord. He will take care of the situation as He sees fit.

Step Three: Find serenity.

I agree with the message of the serenity prayer that one pathway to peace is to control what we can control and to leave the rest to God. Sometimes there is a thin line between what we can control and things that we cannot. If we ask God for wisdom on this matter, we will get it and experience peace.

Step Four: Choose to love anyway.

It goes against our nature as human beings to endure difficult relationships. However, God's grace can empower us to endure very difficult relationships and manifest agape. Pray for God's

Spirit to fill you daily with His love for the difficult people in your life. Trust God that you will receive grace.

Step Five: Stop complaining and reframe your perspective.

When challenges emerge in our lives, there is a tendency to grumble and complain. Instead of complaining, find something or someone to be grateful for. In other words, reframe your perspective on that situation. A great place to start is to be grateful that, "… all things work together for good to those who love God, to those who are the called according to His purpose" (Romans 8:28).

There is something good in every experience – a lesson for us to learn. We must challenge ourselves to have a godly perspective of every person and situation. Sometimes God changes a person and a situation. The other times He changes us, and that makes all the difference in the world.

Step Six: Decide that no one is going to steal your joy.

Regardless of what is happening in your life, make the decision that you will not allow anyone or anything to steal your joy. The joy of the Lord is our strength (See Nehemiah 8:10). His joy will give you the power to endure the most difficult relationships in your life.

Step Seven: Let God be your everything.

Let God fill the voids in your heart so that you do not seek to fulfill them in your relationships. God is our Teacher, Counselor, Healer, Parent, Provider, Friend – everything we need. When you are angry about something in a relationship, pray and ask yourself, *"What do I desire from this person or in this situation?"* Once you discern what you desire, ask God to meet your needs and fulfill the desires of your heart. This will allow us to come to our relationships with a full cup and not an empty one.

Step Eight: Recognize that God has multiple ways of blessing us.

God has multiple people and ways to bless, encourage, and provide for us. We do not need to depend on one relationship or one person as if God cannot bless our lives without them. Seek meaningful relationships with a variety of people and trust He will bless you as He chooses.

Step Nine: Enlist the support of others.

Gather a list of the "balcony" people in your life. These are the people who are your greatest encouragers and supporters. They are also wise people who live in accordance with the Word of God. Let this be the group of people you seek counsel from in times of need.

Step Ten: Stay in the present.

Practice staying in the moment. Jesus said, sufficient today is its own troubles (See Matthew 6:34). We need God's grace to not obsess about the future or the past and to live in the present. Ask God for the grace to focus on living in the moment. He will give you the strength, grace, and power to endure.

For those who are in an abusive relationship, love enduring all things does not extend to allowing yourself and your children to remain in a dangerous situation. Seek help if you are in an abusive situation.

Chapter 10
Live Like You Are Loved

This book has extensively dealt with loving others, but now I want to turn our attention to God's love for us.

In 1 John 4:10, we read: "In this is love, not that we loved God, but that He loved us and sent His Son to be the propitiation for our sins." We learn from this text that God is the initiator of loving us. It is by experiencing and being rooted in His personal love for us (See Ephesians 3:14-19) that, by His Spirit, we can love others as He loves us. God wants us to experience, understand, and be changed by His love so that we can be vessels of agape in the world.

God does not want us to just have an intellectual understanding of His love for us. According to Ephesians 3:14-19, He wants us to experience His love personally. God will take us on a journey of experiencing His love so that nothing or no one can compete with His amazing love for us. So, do you feel like you are loved by God? Do you live like you are loved? When we live from a place of love, then there is an overflow of love in our hearts, which we use to love others. This enables us to love, whether we receive it back or not, because we are overflowing in His love for us.

Here are some steps you can take to go deeper into experiencing God's love for you:

Step One: Journey through the Word of God.

The Bible is God's love story to us. Daily spend time in God's Word. Christ, the Father, and the Holy Spirit will meet with you in the pages of Scripture. As you pray daily and seek His presence in His Word, you will experience God's personal love for you.

Step Two: Confess any sins.

God has already accepted and forgiven us through Christ. However, it is important to confess our sins so that there is nothing that hinders our ability to hear from the Holy Spirit.

Step Three: Look at God's resume.

How has God shown His love to you in the past? Ask God to help you to recall even the small ways He has demonstrated His personal love for you. Also, evaluate the present. How has God shown His love for you recently? Everything that God has done and is doing in your life is a part of His love resume. Ask God to open your eyes to see His love for you clearly. He will show you.

Step Four: Develop a friendship with God.

God desires a friendship with us. Ask God for the ability to honor Him as God and Friend. We can walk with Him, in friendship and love, knowing our sins are all removed through the blood of Christ.

Finally, read *The Father's Love Letter* and listen to it as well on www.fathersloveletter.com. It is a powerful reminder of our Father's love for us. I have included it below (The Scriptures for each statement in the letter is included on their website):

Father's Love Letter

"My Child, you may not know Me, but I know everything about you. I know when you sit down and when you rise up. I am familiar with all your ways. Even the very hairs on your head are numbered. For you were made in My image. In Me you live and move and have your being, for you are My offspring. I knew you even before you were conceived. I chose you when I planned creation. You were not a mistake, for all your days are written in My book. I determined the exact time of your birth and where you would live. You are fearfully and wonderfully made. I knit you together in your mother's womb and brought you forth on the day you were born.

I have been misrepresented by those who don't know Me. I am not distant and angry but am the complete expression of love. And it is My desire to lavish My love on you, simply because you are My child, and I am your Father. I offer you more than your earthly father ever could, for I am the perfect Father. Every good gift that you receive comes from My hand. For I am your provider, and I meet all your needs. My plan for your future has always been filled with hope because I love you with an everlasting love. My thoughts toward you are countless as the sand on the seashore. And I rejoice over you with singing.

I will never stop doing good to you, for you are my treasured possession. I desire to establish you with all My heart and all My soul. And I want to show you great and marvelous things. If you seek Me with all your heart, you will find Me. Delight in Me, and I will give you the desires of your heart. For it is I who gave you those desires. I am able to do more for you than you could possibly imagine. For I am your greatest encourager.

I am also the Father who comforts you in all your troubles. When you are brokenhearted, I am close to you. As a shepherd carries a lamb, I have carried you close to My heart. One day I will wipe away every tear from your eyes and I'll take away all the pain you have suffered on this earth. I am your Father, and I love you even as I love My Son, Jesus. For in Jesus, My love for you is revealed. He is the exact representation of My being. He came to demonstrate that I am for you, not against you and to tell you that I am not counting your sins. Jesus died so that you and I could be reconciled.

His death was the ultimate expression of My love for you. I gave up everything I loved that I might gain your love. If you receive the gift of My Son, Jesus, you receive me and nothing will ever separate you from My love again. Come home, and I'll throw the biggest party heaven has ever seen. I have always been your Father and will always be Father.

My question is ... Will you be My child? I am waiting for you.

Love,

Your Dad Almighty God" [18]

---

[18] https://www.fathersloveletter.com

The Prodigal Son Story

Another expression of the Father's love can be seen in the story of the Prodigal Son. Most of us have heard this story so many times that it may seem a little cliché. However, the story shows a magnanimous picture of our Father's love – the love He wants you and I to experience and to give.

While there are several ways we can view this text, there are two messages in the story that stands out. Middle Eastern culture is one in which both honor and shame play a key role. For instance, if you are a child of someone in that culture, and you disgrace your parents, it could lead to your potential death. In essence, to bring shame on your family would not be tolerated.

In this story, the son asked for his inheritance early, which would have been a shameful thing to do. Then later in the story, we read of the father running towards his "disgraced" son. Culturally for a middle-aged man to run was shameful as well. When Jesus told this story, He may have been referencing the cross, which was an instrument of shame. This is the first message that stands out. Christ endured the shame of the cross on our behalf so that we would understand how much we are loved (See Hebrews 12:2).

The second message that really stands out in the story is the picture of our Father (through the father in the story). The story teaches us that God, our Father, is patient, loving, and quick to forgive when we repent. The father did not reject his estranged son. He embraced and welcomed him home. While in the Prodigal's culture, he was a disgraced son, his father saw him differently (we see this in the father's embracing and kissing of his beloved son). The story ends with the father's love for his son culminating in a lavish party to celebrate his return.

Our heavenly Father's lavish love for us is on full display in this story. We see a picture of not only how He responds to our repentance, but what He feels about us at His core – love! Agape is illustrated beautifully in this story.

Love is patient: We see the father's patience with his son in how he responded upon his return. The farther displayed no anger or resentment towards his son. Instead, he met his son with love. The father was quick to forgive his son so he could continue his relationship with him in spite of his past behavior. The same is true of our Heavenly Father. He is quick to forgive and slow to anger. When we repent of our sins, our Father, and all of heaven, rejoices.

Love is kind: The father demonstrated outrageous kindness to his returning son. He had "the best robe" put on him. He had a ring placed on his finger and sandals placed on his feet. A "fattened calf" was killed for a party that was given in his honor. Our Father's heart is so filled with love for us. He desires true repentance and a genuine desire for a changed life through His Son. Then get ready for His goodness and mercy to follow you all the days of your life.

Rejoices with the Truth: The entire behavior of the father toward his son showed how much he rejoiced with truth. From the initial moments he first saw his son to dealing with his older son, the father demonstrated that living in accordance with truth was a priority for him. Oh, how our Father loves when we acknowledge truth and live by it. He rejoices with truth because He is the Father of Truth.

Love bears all things: The older brother wanted to focus on his brother's sins. However, the father sought to cover the sins of his lost son by celebrating the fact that he was repentant and returned home. Some believe that even the protective nature of love is seen when the father runs out to meet his son. It is believed that the father may have run to his son to protect him from anyone who may have wanted to harm him (because of the shame he caused). Our Father takes no pleasure in revealing our sins to others or focusing on them. His hope is that we would humble ourselves before Him, repent, and confess our sins to Him.

Love believes all things: While the son had come to a place where he knew his behavior toward his father was wrong, he had not yet communicated it to his father. However, because the father thought the best of his son, he knew his son had repented without his son saying a word. Our heavenly Father believes in us and what His grace through Christ can do in our lives. He does not believe the worst about you. He believes the best.

Love hopes all things: The Prodigal Son's father must have maintained hope during his son's absence, that one day he would return. He seemed to have had a vibrant hope that waited patiently and confidently for his son to repent and come home. Our Father focuses on what is good about each of us. In regard to the sinful areas of our lives, He hopes that we will respond to His grace through Christ to change the sinful areas of our lives.

Love endures all things: The father still wanted to have a relationship with his son, even though he acted disgracefully. He was not going to give up on his son no matter what. Love does not give up on others. God never gives up on us. His love is enduring. His love does not quit loving us.

Love never fails: What a mighty God we serve that His love stays and abides with us, even in the midst of our sins, foolishness, pride, and our ignorance. God does not possess a fickle love that is here today and gone tomorrow, nor does God change. Therefore, He will never change His mind about lavishing His amazing love upon us. Amen.

What a beautiful portrait of our loving heavenly Father Jesus painted in this story. Let us love others likewise.

Consider all the attributes of love that we have talked about throughout this book. Ask God which quality of love (that you are weak in) does He want to work on first in your life. Then allow Him to lead you from there. Do not worry about where you are on the journey. God's grace is sufficient to help you, and His power is made perfect in your weakness (See 2 Corinthians 12:9). Commit to being alive to God every day and love the agape way.

About the Author

 Camille has been teaching and preaching the Word of God since she was in high school. God's Word has been the inspiration of her life, throughout her life. It is Camille's mission to give back what God has given to her by inspiring Christians to be transformed by God's Word!

Her business, *Camille Inspires*, is focused on teaching Christian women how to understand and apply God's Word in taking care of their bodies, emotions, and spirit. Camille is a firm believer that there is no problem that God and His Word cannot solve, and she inspires women to believe the same.

As a Certified Lifestyle Coach, she uses the powerful combination of coaching techniques with the Word of God to guide women to the One who transforms lives. Camille and her best friend, Chris, who happens to be her husband, reside in Sunny Florida.

For more information or to contact Camille:
Visit www.CamilleInspires.com.

Notes